D1324316

Because 'God' is infinite, nobody can have the last word.

3 5 7 9 10 8 6 4 2

Vintage
20 Vauxhall Bridge Road,
London SW1V 2SA

Vintage Classics is part of the Penguin Random House
group of companies whose addresses can be found at
global.penguinrandomhouse.com

 Penguin
Random House
UK

Extracts from *The Case for God* copyright © Karen Armstrong 2009; *Fields of Blood* copyright © Karen Armstrong 2014; *The Lost Art of Scripture* copyright © Karen Armstrong 2019

Karen Armstrong has asserted her right to be identified as the author of this Work in accordance with the Copyright, Designs and Patents Act 1988

The Case for God first published in Great Britain by The Bodley Head in 2009
First published in Vintage in 2010
Fields of Blood first published in Great Britain by The Bodley Head in 2014
First published in Vintage in 2015
The Lost Art of Scripture first published in Great Britain by The Bodley Head in 2019

This short edition published by Vintage in 2019

penguin.co.uk/vintage

A CIP catalogue record for this book is available from the British Library

ISBN 9781784875695

Typeset in 10.5/14.5 pt FreightText Pro by Jouve (UK), Milton Keynes
Printed and bound in Great Britain by Clays Ltd, Elcograf S.p.A.

Penguin Random House is committed to a sustainable future for our business, our readers and our planet. This book is made from Forest Stewardship Council® certified paper.

MIX
Paper from
responsible sources
FSC® C018179
www.fsc.org

Religion

KAREN ARMSTRONG

VINTAGE MINIS

Contents

What is 'Religion'?

WE ARE TALKING far too much about God these days and what we say is often facile. In our democratic society, we think that the concept of God *should* be easy and that religion ought to be readily accessible to anybody. 'That book was really hard!' readers have told me reproachfully, shaking their heads in faint reproof. 'Of course it was!' I want to reply. 'It was about God.' But many find this puzzling. Surely everybody knows what God is: the Supreme Being, a divine Personality, who created the world and everything in it. They look perplexed if you point out that it is inaccurate to call God the Supreme Being because God is not *a* being at all, and that we really don't know what we mean when we say that he is 'good', 'wise' or 'intelligent'. People of faith know in theory that God is utterly transcendent, but they seem sometimes to assume that *they* know exactly who 'he' is and what he thinks, loves and expects. We tend to tame and domesticate God's 'otherness'. We regularly ask God to bless our nation, save our queen, cure our sickness or give us a fine day for the picnic. We remind God that he has created the world and that we are miserable sinners, as though this may have slipped his mind. Politicians quote God to justify their policies; teachers use him to keep order in the classroom; and terrorists commit atrocities in his name. We beg God to support 'our' side in an election or a war, even though our opponents are, presumably, also God's children and the object of his love and care.

There is also a tendency to assume that, even though we now live in a totally transformed world and have an entirely different world-view, people have always thought about God in exactly the same way as we do today. But despite our scientific and technological brilliance, our religious thinking is sometimes remarkably undeveloped, even primitive. In some ways the modern God resembles the High God of remote antiquity, a theology that was unanimously either jettisoned or radically reinterpreted because it was found to be inept. Many people in the pre-modern world knew that it was very difficult indeed to speak about God.

Theology is, of course, a very wordy discipline. People have written reams and talked unstoppably about God. But some of the greatest Jewish, Christian and Muslim theologians made it clear that while it was important to put our ideas about the divine into words, these doctrines were man-made and, therefore, were bound to be inadequate. They devised spiritual exercises that deliberately subverted normal patterns of thought and speech to help the faithful understand that the words we use to describe mundane things were simply not suitable for God. 'He' was not good, divine, powerful or intelligent in any way that we could understand. We could not even say that God 'existed', because our concept of existence was too limited. Some of the sages preferred to say that God was 'Nothing' because God was not another being. You certainly could not read your scriptures literally, as if they referred to divine facts. To these theologians some of our modern ideas about God would have seemed idolatrous.

It was not just a few radical theologians who took this line. Symbolism came more naturally to people in the pre-modern world than it does to us today. In medieval Europe, for example, Christians were taught to see the Mass as a symbolic re-enactment of Jesus' life, death and resurrection. The fact that they could not follow the Latin added to its mystique. Much of the Mass was recited by the priest in an undertone and the solemn silence and liturgical drama, with its music and stylised gestures, put the congregation into a mental 'space' that was separate from ordinary life. Today many are able to own a copy of the Bible or the Qur'an and have the literacy to read them, but in the past most people had an entirely different relationship with their scriptures. They listened to them, recited piecemeal, often in a foreign language and always in a heightened liturgical context. Preachers instructed them not to understand these texts in a purely literal way and suggested figurative interpretations. In the 'mystery plays' performed annually on the feast of Corpus Christi, medievals felt free to change the biblical stories, add new characters and transpose them into a contemporary setting. These tales were not historical in our sense, because they were *more* than history.

In most pre-modern cultures, there were two recognised ways of thinking, speaking and acquiring knowledge. The Greeks called them *mythos* and *logos*. Both were essential and neither was considered superior to the other; they were not in conflict but complementary. Each had its own sphere of competence and it was considered unwise to mix the two. *Logos* ('reason') was the pragmatic mode of thought that enabled people to function effectively in the world. It had, therefore, to correspond accurately to external reality. People have always needed *logos* to make an efficient weapon, organise their societies or plan an expedition. *Logos* was forward-looking, continually on the lookout for new ways of controlling the environment, improving old insights or inventing something fresh. *Logos* was essential to the survival of our species. But it had its limitations: it could not assuage human grief or find ultimate meaning in life's struggles. For that, people turned to *mythos* or 'myth'.

Today we live in a society of scientific *logos* and myth has fallen into disrepute. In popular parlance, a 'myth' is something that is not true. But in the past, myth was not self-indulgent fantasy; rather, like *logos*, it helped people to live creatively in our confusing world, though in a different way. Myths may have told stories about the gods, but they were really focused on the more elusive, puzzling and tragic aspects of the human predicament that lay outside the remit of *logos*. Myth has been called a primitive form of psychology. When a myth described heroes threading their way through labyrinths, descending into the underworld or fighting monsters, these were not understood as primarily factual stories. They were designed to help people negotiate the obscure regions of the psyche, which are difficult to access but which profoundly influence our thought and behaviour. People had to enter the warren of their own minds and fight their personal demons. When Freud and Jung began to chart their scientific search for the soul, they instinctively turned to these ancient myths. A myth was never intended as an accurate account of a historical event; it was *something that had in some sense happened once but that also happens all the time.*

But a myth would not be effective if people simply 'believed' in it. It was essentially a programme of action. It could put you in the correct spiritual or psychological posture but it was up to you to take the next step and make the 'truth' of the myth a reality in your own life. The only way to assess the value and truth of any myth was to act upon it. The myth of the hero, for example, which takes the same form in nearly all cultural traditions, taught people how to unlock their own heroic potential. Later, the stories of historical figures such as the Buddha, Jesus or Muhammad were made to conform to this paradigm so that their followers could imitate them in the same way. Put into practice, a myth could tell us something profoundly true about our humanity. It showed us how to live more richly and intensely, how to cope with our mortality, and how to endure the suffering that flesh is heir to. But if we failed to apply it to our situation, a myth would remain abstract and incredible. From a very early date, people re-enacted their myths in stylised ceremonies that worked aesthetically upon participants and, like any work of art, introduced them to a deeper dimension of existence. Myth and ritual were thus inseparable, so much so that it is often a matter of scholarly debate which came first: the mythical story or the rites attached to it. Without ritual, myths made no sense and would remain as opaque as a musical score, which is impenetrable to most of us until interpreted instrumentally.

Religion, therefore, was not primarily something that people thought but something they did. Its truth was acquired by practical action. It is no use imagining that you will be able to drive a car if you simply read the manual or study the Highway Code. You cannot learn to dance, paint or cook by perusing texts or recipes. The rules of a board game sound obscure, unnecessarily complicated and dull until you start to play, when everything falls into place. There are some things that can only be learned by constant, dedicated practice, but if you persevere you find that you achieve something that seemed initially impossible. Instead of sinking to the bottom of the pool, you can float. You may learn to jump higher and with more grace than seems humanly possible, or sing with unearthly beauty. You do not always understand how you achieve these feats, because your mind directs your body in a way that bypasses conscious, logical deliberation. But somehow you learn to transcend your original capabilities. Some of these activities bring indescribable joy. A musician can lose herself in her music, a dancer becomes inseparable from the dance, and a skier feels entirely at one with himself and the external world as he speeds down the slope. It is a satisfaction that goes deeper than merely 'feeling good'. It is what the Greeks called *ekstasis*, a 'stepping outside' the norm.

Religion is a practical discipline that teaches us to discover new capacities of mind and heart. It is no use magisterially weighing up the teachings of religion to judge their truth or falsehood, before embarking on a religious way of life. You will only discover their truth – or lack of it – if you translate these doctrines into ritual or ethical action. Like any skill, religion requires perseverance, hard work and discipline. Some people will be better at it than others, some appallingly inept, and others will miss the point entirely. But those who do not apply themselves will get nowhere at all. Religious people find it hard to explain how their rituals and practices work, just as a skater may not be fully conscious of the physical laws that enable her to soar over the ice on a thin blade.

The early Daoists saw religion as a 'knack' acquired by constant practice. Zhuangzi (c.370–311 BCE), one of the most important figures in the spiritual history of China, explained that it was no good trying to analyse religious teachings logically. He cites the carpenter Bian: 'When I work on a wheel, if I hit too softly, pleasant as this is, it doesn't make for a good wheel. If I hit it furiously, I get tired and the thing doesn't work! So not too soft, not too vigorous. I grasp it in my hand and hold it in my heart. I cannot express this by word of mouth, I just know it.' A hunchback who trapped cicadas in the forest with a sticky pole never missed a single one. He had so perfected his powers of concentration that he lost himself in the task, and his hands seemed to move by themselves. He had no idea how he did it, but knew only that he had acquired the knack after months of practice. This self-forgetfulness, Zhuangzi explained, was an *ekstasis* that enabled you to 'step outside' the prism of ego and experience the divine.

People who acquired this knack discovered a transcendent dimension of life that was not simply an external reality 'out there' but was identical with the deepest level of their being. This reality, which they have called God, Dao, Brahman or Nirvana, has been a fact of human life. But it was impossible to explain what it was in terms of *logos*. This imprecision was not frustrating, as a modern Western person might imagine, but brought with it an *ekstasis* that lifted practitioners beyond the constricting confines of self. Our scientifically oriented knowledge seeks to master reality, explain it, and bring it under the control of reason, but a delight in unknowing has also been part of the human experience. Even today, poets, philosophers, mathematicians and scientists find that the contemplation of the insoluble is a source of joy, astonishment and contentment.

One of the peculiar characteristics of the human mind is its ability to have ideas and experiences that exceed our conceptual grasp. We constantly push our thoughts to an extreme, so that our minds seem to elide naturally into an apprehension of transcendence. Music has always been inseparable from religious expression, because, like religion at its best, music marks the 'limits of reason'. Because a territory is defined by its extremities, it follows that music must be 'definitively' rational. It is the most corporeal of the arts: it is produced by breath, voice, horsehair, shells, guts and skins and reaches 'resonances in our bodies at levels deeper than will or consciousness'. But it is also highly cerebral, requiring the balance of intricately complex energies and form relations, and is intimately connected with mathematics. Yet this intensely rational activity segues into transcendence. Music goes beyond the reach of words: it is not *about* anything. A late Beethoven quartet does not represent sorrow but elicits it in hearer and player alike; and yet it is emphatically not a sad experience. Like tragedy, it brings intense pleasure and insight. We seem to experience sadness directly in a way that transcends ego, because this is not *my* sadness but sorrow itself. In music, therefore, subjective and objective become one. Language has limits that we cannot cross. When we listen critically to our stuttering attempts to express ourselves, we become aware of an inexpressible otherness. 'It is decisively the fact that language does have frontiers,' explains the British critic George Steiner, 'that gives proof of a transcendent presence in the fabric of the world. It is just because we can go no further, because speech so marvellously fails us, that we experience the certitude of a divine meaning surpassing and enfolding ours.' Every day, music confronts us with a mode of knowledge that defies logical analysis and empirical proof. It is 'brimful of meanings which will not translate into logical structures or verbal expression'. Hence all art constantly aspires to the condition of music; so too, at its best, does theology.

A modern sceptic will find it impossible to accept Steiner's conclusion that 'What lies beyond man's word is eloquent of God.' But perhaps that is because we have too limited an idea of God. We have not been doing our practice and have lost the 'knack' of religion. During the sixteenth and seventeenth centuries, a period that historians call the early modern period, Western people began to develop an entirely new kind of civilisation, governed by scientific rationality and based economically on technology and capital investment. *Logos* achieved such spectacular results that myth was discredited and the scientific method was thought to be the only reliable means of attaining truth. This would make religion difficult, if not impossible. As theologians began to adopt the criteria of science, the *mythoi* of Christianity were interpreted as empirically, rationally and historically verifiable and forced into a style of thinking that was alien to them. Philosophers and scientists could no longer see the point of ritual, and religious knowledge became theoretical rather than practical. We lost the art of interpreting the old tales of gods walking the earth, dead men striding out of tombs, or seas parting miraculously. We began to understand concepts such as faith, revelation, myth, mystery and dogma in a way that would have been very surprising to our ancestors. In particular, the meaning of the word 'belief' changed, so that a credulous acceptance of creedal doctrines became the prerequisite of faith, so much so that today we often speak of religious people as 'believers' as though accepting orthodox dogma 'on faith' were their most important activity.

This rationalised interpretation of religion has resulted in two distinctively modern phenomena: fundamentalism and atheism. The two are related. The defensive piety popularly known as 'fundamentalism' erupted in almost every major faith during the twentieth century. In their desire to produce a wholly rational, scientific faith that abolished *mythos* in favour of *logos*, Christian fundamentalists have interpreted scripture with a literalism that is unparalleled in the history of religion. In the United States,

Protestant fundamentalists have evolved an ideology known as 'creation science', which regards the *mythoi* of the Bible as scientifically accurate. They have, therefore, campaigned against the teaching of evolution in the public schools, because it contradicts the creation story in the first chapter of Genesis.

Historically atheism has rarely been a blanket denial of the sacred per se but has nearly always rejected a particular conception of the divine. At an early stage of their history, Christians and Muslims were both called 'atheists' by their pagan contemporaries, not because they denied the reality of God but because their conception of divinity was so different that it seemed blasphemous. Atheism is therefore parasitically dependent on the form of theism it seeks to eliminate and becomes its reverse mirror image. Classical Western atheism was developed during the nineteenth and early twentieth centuries by Feuerbach, Marx, Nietzsche and Freud, whose ideology was essentially a response to and dictated by the theological perception of God that had developed in Europe and the United States during the modern period. The more recent atheism of Richard Dawkins, Christopher Hitchens and Sam Harris is rather different, because it has focused exclusively on the God developed by the fundamentalisms, and all three insist that fundamentalism constitutes the essence and core of all religion. This has weakened their critique, because fundamentalism is in fact a defiantly unorthodox form of faith that frequently misrepresents the tradition it is trying to defend. But the 'new atheists' command a wide readership, not only in secular Europe but even in the more conventionally religious United States. The popularity of their books suggests that many people are bewildered and even angered by the God concept they have inherited.

It is a pity that Dawkins, Hitchens and Harris express themselves so intemperately, because some of their criticisms are valid. Religious people have indeed committed atrocities and crimes, and the fundamentalist theology the new atheists attack is indeed 'unskilful', as the Buddhists would say. But they refuse, on principle, to dialogue with theologians who are more representative of mainstream tradition. As a result, their analysis is disappointingly shallow, because it is based on such poor theology. In fact, the new atheists are not radical enough. Jewish, Christian and Muslim theologians have insisted for centuries that God does not exist and that there is 'nothing' out there; in making these assertions their aim was not to deny the reality of God but to safeguard God's transcendence. But in our talkative and highly opinionated society, we seem to have lost sight of this important tradition, which could solve many of our current religious problems.

I have no intention of attacking anybody's sincerely held beliefs. Many thousands of people find that the symbolism of the modern God works well for them: backed up by inspiring rituals and the discipline of living in a vibrant community, it has given them a sense of transcendent meaning. All the world faiths insist that true spirituality must be expressed consistently in practical compassion, the ability to *feel with* the other. If a conventional idea of God inspires empathy and respect for all others, it is doing its job. But the modern God is only one of the many theologies that developed during the three-thousand-year history of monotheism. Because 'God' is infinite, nobody can have the last word.

Even though so many people are antagonistic to faith, the world is currently experiencing a religious revival. Contrary to the confident secularist predictions of the mid twentieth century, religion is not going to disappear. But if it succumbs to the violent and intolerant strain that has always been inherent not only in monotheism but also in the modern scientific ethos, the new religiosity will be 'unskilful'. We are seeing a great deal of strident dogmatism today, religious and secular, but there is also a growing appreciation of the value of unknowing. We can never recreate the past, but we can learn from its mistakes and insights. There is a long religious tradition that stressed the importance of recognising the limits of our knowledge, of silence, reticence and awe. One of the conditions of enlightenment has always been a willingness to let go of what we thought we knew in order to appreciate truths we had never dreamed of. We may have to unlearn a great deal about religion before we can move on to new understanding.

God and Man

FOR ABOUT FIFTY years now it has been clear in the academy that there is no universal way to define religion. In the West we see 'religion' as a coherent system of obligatory beliefs, institutions and rituals, centring on a supernatural God, whose practice is essentially private and hermetically sealed off from all 'secular' activities. But words in other languages that we translate as 'religion' almost invariably refer to something larger, vaguer and more encompassing. The Arabic *din* signifies a whole way of life. The Sanskrit *dharma* is also 'a "total" concept, untranslatable, which covers law, justice, morals, and social life'. The *Oxford Classical Dictionary* firmly states: 'No word in either Greek or Latin corresponds to the English "religion" or "religious."' The idea of religion as a personal and systematic pursuit was entirely absent from classical Greece, Japan, Egypt, Mesopotamia, Iran, China and India. Nor does the Hebrew Bible have any abstract concept of religion; and the Talmudic rabbis would have found it impossible to express what they meant by faith in a single word or even in a formula, since the Talmud was expressly designed to bring the whole of human life into the ambit of the sacred.

The origins of the Latin *religio* are obscure. It was not 'a great objective something' but had imprecise connotations of obligation and taboo; to say that a cultic observance, a family propriety or keeping an oath was *religio* for you meant that it was incumbent on you to do it. The word acquired an important new meaning among early Christian theologians: an attitude of reverence towards God and the universe as a whole. For St Augustine (*c.* 354–430 BCE), *religio* was neither a system of rituals and doctrines nor a historical institutionalised tradition but a personal encounter with the transcendence that we call God as well as the bond that unites us to the divine and to one another. In medieval Europe, *religio* came to refer to the monastic life and distinguished the monk from the 'secular' priest, someone who lived and worked in the world (*saeculum*).

The only faith tradition that does fit the modern Western notion of religion as something codified and private is Protestant Christianity, which, like 'religion' in this sense of the word is also a product of the early modern period. At this time Europeans and Americans had begun to separate religion and politics, because they assumed, not altogether accurately, that the theological squabbles of the Reformation had been entirely responsible for the Thirty Years War. The conviction that religion must be rigorously excluded from political life has been called the charter-myth of the sovereign nation state. The philosophers and statesmen who pioneered this dogma believed that they were returning to the more satisfactory state of affairs that had existed before ambitious Catholic clerics had confused two utterly distinct realms. But in fact their secular ideology was as radical an innovation as the modern market economy that the West was concurrently devising. To non-Westerners, who had not been through this particular modernising process, both these innovations would seem unnatural and even incomprehensible. The habit of separating religion and politics is now so routine in the West that it is difficult for us to appreciate how thoroughly the two co-inhered in the past. It was never simply a question of the state 'using' religion; the two were indivisible. Dissociating them would have seemed like trying to extract the gin from a cocktail.

In the pre-modern world, religion permeated all aspects of life. We shall see that a host of activities now considered mundane were experienced as deeply sacred: forest-clearing, hunting, football matches, dice games, astronomy, farming, state-building, tugs of war, town planning, commerce, imbibing strong drink, and, most particularly, warfare. Ancient peoples would have found it impossible to see where 'religion' ended and 'politics' began. This was not because they were too stupid to understand the distinction but because they wanted to invest everything they did with ultimate value. We are meaning-seeking creatures and, unlike other animals, fall very easily into despair if we fail to make sense of our lives. We find the prospect of our inevitable extinction hard to bear. We are troubled by natural disasters and human cruelty and acutely aware of our physical and psychological frailty. We find it astonishing that we are here at all and want to know why. We also have a great capacity for wonder. Ancient philosophies were entranced by the order of the cosmos; they marvelled at the mysterious power that kept the heavenly bodies in their orbits, the seas within bounds and ensured that the earth regularly came to life again after the dearth of winter, and they longed to participate in this richer and more permanent existence.

They expressed this yearning in terms of what is known as the perennial philosophy, so-called because it was present, in some form, in most premodern cultures. Every single person, object or experience was seen as a replica, a pale shadow, of a reality that was stronger and more enduring than anything in their ordinary experience but which they only glimpsed in visionary moments or in dreams. By ritually imitating what they understood to be the gestures and actions of their celestial alter egos – whether gods, ancestors or culture heroes – pre-modern folk felt themselves to be caught up in their larger dimension of existence. We humans are profoundly artificial and tend naturally towards archetypes and paradigms. We constantly strive to improve on nature or approximate to an ideal that transcends the day-to-day. Even our contemporary cult of celebrity can be understood as an expression of our reverence for and yearning to emulate models of 'super-humanity'. Feeling ourselves connected to such extraordinary realities satisfies an essential craving. It touches us within, lifts us momentarily beyond ourselves, so that we seem to inhabit our humanity more fully than usual and feel in touch with the deeper currents of life. If we no longer find this experience in a church or temple, we seek it in art, a musical concert, sex, drugs – or warfare. What this last may have to do with these other moments of transport may not be so obvious but it is one of the oldest triggers of ecstatic experience. To understand why, it will be helpful to consider the development of our neuro-anatomy.

The imagination has been the cause of our major

achievements in science and technology as well as in art and religion. Neurologists tell us that in fact we have no direct contact with the world we inhabit. We have only perspectives that come to us through the intricate circuits of our nervous system, so that we all – scientists as well as mystics – know only representations of reality, not reality itself. We deal with the world as it appears to us, not as it intrinsically is, so some of our interpretations may be more accurate than others. This somewhat disturbing news means that the 'objective truths' on which we rely are inherently illusive. The world is *there*; its energy and form exist. But our apprehension of it is only a mental projection. The world is outside our bodies, but not outside our minds. 'We *are* this little universe,' the Benedictine mystic Bede Griffiths (1906–93) explained, 'a microcosm in which the macrocosm is present as a hologram.' We are surrounded by a reality that transcends – or 'goes beyond' – our conceptual grasp.

What we regard as truth, therefore, is inescapably bound up with a world that we construct for ourselves. As soon as the first humans learned to manipulate tools, they created works of art to make sense of the terror, wonder and mystery of their existence. From the very beginning, art was inextricably bound up with what we call 'religion', which is itself an art form. The Lascaux Caves, a cultic site since 17,000 BCE, are decorated with numinous paintings of local wildlife, and nearby, in the underground labyrinth of Trois Frères at Ariège, there are spectacular engravings of mammoths, bison, wolverines and musk-oxen. Dominating the scene is a massive painted figure, half man, half beast, who fixes his huge, penetrating eyes on visitors as they stumble out of the underground tunnel that provides the only route to this prehistoric temple. This hybrid creature transcends anything in our empirical experience but seems to reflect a sense of the underlying unity of animal, human and divine.

There is no specific 'God-spot' in the human brain that yields a sense of the sacred. But in recent decades, neurologists have discovered that the right hemisphere of the brain is essential to the creation of poetry, music and religion. It is involved with the formation of our sense of self and has a broader, less focused mode of attention than the left hemisphere which is more pragmatic and selective. Above all, it sees itself as connected to the outside world, whereas the left hemisphere holds aloof from it. Specialising in language, analysis and problem-solving, the left side of our brain suppresses information that it cannot grasp conceptually. The right hemisphere, however, whose functions tended in the past to be overlooked by scientists, has a holistic rather than an analytical vision; it sees each thing in relation to the

whole and perceives the interconnectedness of reality. It is, therefore, at home with metaphor, in which
disparate entities become one while the left hemisphere tends to be literal and to wrest things from
their context so that it can categorise and make use
of them. News reaches the right hemisphere first,
where it appears as part of an interlocking unity;
it then passes to the left hemisphere, where it is
defined, analysed and its use assessed. But the left
can produce only a reductive version of complex
reality, and once processed, this information is
passed back to the right hemisphere, where we see
it – insofar as we can – in the context of the whole.

Our modern focus on the empirical and objective
insights provided by the left hemisphere has unques-
tionably been of immense benefit to humanity. It has
expanded our mental and physical horizons, dra-
matically enhanced our understanding of the world,
has greatly reduced human suffering, and enabled
more people than ever before to experience physical
and emotional well-being. Hence, modern education
tends increasingly to privilege the scientific endeavour and marginalise what we call the humanities.
This, however, is regrettable because it means that
we are in danger of cultivating only half of our mental
capacities fully. Just as it would be insane to ignore
the logic, analysis and rationality produced by the
left hemisphere, psychologists and neurologists tell

us that to function creatively and safely in the world, its activities must be integrated with those of the right.

The left brain is by nature competitive; largely ignorant of the work of the right, it tends to be over-confident. The right hemisphere, however, has a more comprehensive vision of reality, which, as we have seen, we can never grasp fully; it is more at home with embodiment and the physical than the left. The left brain is essential to our survival and enables us to investigate and master our environment, but it can offer us only an abstract representation of the complex information it receives from the right. Because the right hemisphere is less self-centred, it is more realistic than the left hemisphere. Its wide-ranging vision enables it to hold different views of reality simultaneously and, unlike the left, it does not form certainties based on abstraction. Pro-foundly attuned to the Other – to everything that is not ourselves – the right hemisphere is alert to rela-tionships. It is the seat of empathy, pathos and our sense of justice. Because it can see an-other point of view, it inhibits our natural selfishness.

The two sides of our brain normally work in tandem and their functions are closely interwined, but in some periods of history, people have tended to cultivate one more than the other. Until recently, for example, neuroscientists referred to the right hemisphere as the 'minor' hemisphere, betraying our modern preference for analytic and propositional thought. But throughout history, artists, poets and mystics have carefully cultivated the insights of the right hemisphere. Long before the activities of the two sides of the brain had been fully explored, the American philosopher William James (1842–1910) argued that our everyday rational awareness was only one kind of consciousness. There were other modes of perception, separated from it by the flimsiest of screens, where the laws governing our more mundane habits of thought seem to be suspended. James was convinced that to know ourselves fully required the nurturing of the 'peak' experiences that occur when ordinary – or, as we would say now, left-brain – consciousness was in abeyance. We will see that from a very early period, certain gifted individuals have deliberately cultivated what we would now call a right-hemispheric awareness and have had apprehensions of the ineffable unity of reality. Some of these prophets, poets and seers expressed their insights in scripture; others were inspired by scripture to cultivate this awareness. But they were usually careful to integrate these right-brain intuitions with the practical imperatives of the left brain. These people were not freaks, nor were they deluded. They were exercising a natural faculty which brought them important insights that, as we shall see, are essential to humanity.

We humans have a deep-seated yearning for transformation. People did not merely seek an experience of transcendence; rather, they wanted to embody and somehow become one with it. They didn't want a distant deity but sought an enhanced humanity. People want to 'get beyond' suffering and mortality and devise ways of achieving this. Today we are less ambitious; we want to be slimmer, healthier, younger and more attractive than we really are. We feel that a 'better self' lurks beneath our lamentably imperfect one: we want to be kinder, braver, more brilliant and charismatic. The American scholar Frederick Streng has this working definition of religion:

> Religion is a *means of ultimate transformation* . . . An ultimate transformation is a fundamental change from being caught up in the troubles of common existence (sin, ignorance) to living in such a way that one can cope at the deepest level with these troubles. That capacity for living allows one to experience the most authentic or deepest reality – the ultimate.

The myths, rituals, sacred texts and ethical practices of religion develop a plan of action 'whereby people reach beyond themselves to connect with the true and ultimate reality that will save them from the destructive forces of everyday existence'. Living with what is ultimately real and true, people have found that they are not only better able to bear these destructive tensions, but that life itself acquires new depth and purpose.

But what is this 'true and ultimate reality'? We will see that the scriptures have given it various names – *rta*, Brahman, Dao, nirvana, Elohim or God – but in the modern West we have developed an inadequate and ultimately unworkable idea of the divine, which previous generations would have found naïve and immature. As a child, I learned this response to the question 'What is God?' in the Catholic catechism: 'God is the Supreme Spirit, who alone exists of himself, and is infinite in all perfections.' This is not only arid and uninspiring but fundamentally incorrect because it attempts to *define*, a word whose literal meaning is 'to set limits upon', an essentially illimitable reality. We shall see that when the left hemisphere was less cultivated than it is today, what we call 'God' was neither *a* 'spirit' nor *a* 'being'. God was, rather, Reality itself. Not only did God have no gender, but leading theologians and mystics insisted that God did not 'exist' in any way that we can understand. Before the modern period, the 'ultimate reality' came closer to what the German philosopher Martin Heidegger (1899–1976) called 'Being', a fundamental energy that supports and pervades everything that exists. You cannot see, touch or hear it, but can only watch it mysteriously at work in the people, objects and natural forces that it informs. It is essentially indefinable because it is impossible to get outside it and view it objectively.

Traditionally, the sacred was experienced as a presence that permeates the whole of reality – humans, animals, plants, stars, wind and rain. The Romantic poet William Wordsworth (1770–1850) carefully referred to it as 'something' because it was indefinable and, therefore, transcended propositional thought. He had experienced

> a sense sublime
> Of something far more deeply interfused
> Whose dwelling is the light of setting suns
> And the round ocean and the living air,
> And the blue sky and in the mind of man.

He had, he says, 'learned' to acquire this insight. We might say he achieved it by deliberately cultivating a right-hemispheric awareness by – for a limited time – suppressing the analytical activities of the left. When people tried to access the 'ultimate', therefore, they were not submitting to an alien, omnipotent and distant 'being' but were attempting to achieve a more authentic mode of existence. Right up to the early modern period, sages, poets and theologians insisted that what we call 'God', 'Brahman' or 'Dao' was ineffable, indescribable and unknowable – and yet was within them: a constant source of life, energy and inspiration.

Our modern society, however, is rooted in *logos* or 'reason', which must relate precisely to factual, objective and empirical reality if it is to function efficiently in the world. But just as both hemispheres of the brain are necessary for our full functioning, both *mythos* and *logos* are essential to human beings – and both have limitations. Myth cannot bring something entirely new into existence, as *logos* can. A scientist can cure hitherto incurable diseases, but this cannot prevent him from succumbing occasionally to despair when confronted with the mortality, tragedy and apparent pointlessness of our existence.

God and Knowledge

AT THE SECOND International Congress of Mathematicians in Paris in 1900, the German mathematician David Hilbert (1862–1943) confidently predicted a century of unparalleled scientific progress. There were just twenty-three outstanding problems in the Newtonian system, and once these had been solved, our knowledge of the universe would be complete. There appeared to be no limit to modern Western advance. In nearly all fields, artists, scientists and philosophers seemed to anticipate a brave new world. 'In or about December 1910, human nature changed,' wrote the British novelist Virginia Woolf (1882–1941) after visiting the startling exhibition of French Post-Impressionist painters. Artists deliberately flouted their viewers' expectations, tacitly proclaiming the need for a new vision in a new world. Old certainties were evaporating. Some wanted to contemplate irreducible fundamentals, cut out the peripheral and focus on the essential in order to construct a different reality: scientists searched for the atom or the particle; sociologists and anthropologists reverted to primeval societies and primitive artefacts. People wanted to break the past asunder, split the atom to make something new. Pablo Picasso (1881–1973) either dismembered his subjects or viewed them simultaneously from different perspectives. The novels of Woolf and James Joyce (1882–1914) abandoned the traditional narratives of cause and effect, throwing their readers into the chaotic stream of their characters' consciousness, so that they were uncertain about what was actually happening or how they should judge the action.

But the First World War revealed the self-destructive nihilism that, despite its colossal achievements, lurked at the heart of modern Western civilisation. It has been described as the collective suicide of Europe: by slaughtering a generation of young men, the war so damaged European society at its core that arguably it has never fully recovered. The utter futility of trench warfare, fought as it was for no adequate social, ideological or humanitarian cause, defied the rationalism of the scientific age. The most advanced and civilised countries in Europe had crippled themselves and their opponents with their new military technology simply to serve the national ego. The war itself seemed a terrible parody of the mechanical ideal: once the intricate mechanism of conscription, troop transportation and the manufacture of weapons had been switched on, it seemed to acquire its own momentum and proved almost impossible to stop. After the Armistice, the economy of the West seemed in terminal decline, and the 1930s saw the Great Depression and the rise of fascism and communism. By the end of the decade, the unthinkable had happened and the world was embroiled in a second global war. It was now difficult to feel sanguine about the limitless progress of civilisation. Modern secular ideologies were proving to be as lethal as any religious bigotry. They revealed the inherent destructiveness of all idolatry: once the finite reality of the nation had become an absolute value, it was compelled to overcome and destroy all rival claimants.

Modern science had been founded on the belief that it was possible to achieve objective certainty. Hume and Kant had cast doubt on this ideal by suggesting that our understanding of the external world was merely a reflection of human psychology. But even Kant believed that the fundamental categories of Newtonian science – space, time, substance and causality – were beyond question. Yet within a generation of Hilbert's confident prediction that all physicists had to do was add the final touches to Newton's great 'Systeme', it had been superseded.

Already in the late nineteenth century, the Scottish physicist James Clerk-Maxwell (1831–79) had developed the theory of electromagnetic radiation, showing that physicists were beginning to understand time quite differently from the way we experience it, since a radio wave could be received before it had been sent. The puzzling experiments on ether drift and the speed of light conducted by the American scientists Albert Michelson (1852–1951) and Edward Morley (1838–1923) suggested that the relative velocities of light from the sun were the same in the direction of the earth's rotation as when opposed to it, which was entirely inconsistent with Newtonian mechanics. There followed the discovery of radioactivity by Alexander Edmond Becquerel (1820–91) and the isolation of quantum phenomena by Max Planck (1858–1947). Finally, Albert Einstein (1879–1955) applied Planck's quantum theory to light, and formulated his theories of special (1905) and general (1916) relativity. Relativity was able to accommodate the Michelson–Morley findings by merging the concepts of space and time, regarded as absolutes by Newton, into a space–time continuum. Building on Einstein's breakthrough, Niels Bohr (1885–1962) and Werner Heisenberg (1901–76) developed quantum mechanics, an achievement that contradicted nearly every major postulate of Newtonian physics.

So much for the traditional assumption that

knowledge would proceed incrementally, as each generation improved on the achievements of its forebears. In the bewildering universe of quantum mechanics, three-dimensional space and uni-dimensional time had become relative aspects of a four-dimensional space–time continuum. Atoms were not the solid, indestructible building blocks of nature but were found to be largely empty. Time passed at different rates for observers travelling at different speeds: it could go backwards or even stop entirely. Euclid's geometrical laws no longer provided the universal and necessary structure of nature. The planets did not move in their orbits because they were drawn to the sun by gravitational force operating at a distance but because the space in which they moved was actually curved. Subatomic phenomena were particularly baffling because they could be observed as both waves and particles of energy. 'All my attempts to adapt the theoretical foundation of physics to this knowledge failed me,' Einstein recalled. 'It was as if the ground had been pulled out from under me, with no firm foundation to be seen anywhere upon which one could have built.'

If these discoveries were bewildering to scien-tists, they seemed utterly impenetrable to the layman. A curved space, finite and yet unbounded; objects that were not things but merely processes; an expand-ing universe; phenomena that took no definite shape until they were observed – all defied any received presupposition. Newton's grand certainties had been replaced by a system that was ambiguous, shifting and indeterminate. Despite Hilbert, we seemed no closer to understanding the universe. Human beings, randomly produced minutiae whose existence was probably ephemeral, still appeared to be cast adrift in a vast, impersonal universe. There was no clear answer as to what had preceded the 'big bang' that had given birth to the universe. Even physicists did not believe that the equations of quantum theory described what was actually there; these mathematical abstractions could not be put into words and our knowledge was confined to symbols that were mere shadows of an indescribable reality. Unknowing seemed built in to the human condition. The revolution of the 1920s had overturned traditional scientific orthodoxy, and if that had happened once, it could happen again.

Some Christians believed that the new physics was friendly to faith, even though Einstein always insisted that relativity was a scientific theory and had no bearing on religion. They seized eagerly on his famous remark in a debate with Bohr in Brussels (1927) that although quantum mechanics was 'certainly imposing', an 'inner voice tells me that it . . . does not bring us any closer to the secret of the Old One. I, at any rate, am convinced that He does not throw dice.' But Einstein was not referring to the personal God; he had simply used the 'Old One' (a medieval Kabbalistic image) to symbolise the impersonal, intelligible and immanent order of what exists. The British astronomer Arthur Stanley Eddington, however, saw relativity as evidence for the existence of mind in nature; Canon Arthur F. Smethurst regarded it as a manifestation of the Holy Spirit; others saw the new conception of time as validating the afterlife; big bang theory was thought to substantiate the Genesis account; and some even managed to see the indeterminacy of quantum mechanics as support for God's providential control of the world. This type of speculation was ill-conceived. Inured to their need for scientific proof, these apologists were still interpreting the ancient biblical symbols in too literal a manner. Max Planck had a more sage view of the relations between science and religion. The two were quite compatible: science dealt with the objective, material world and religion with values and ethics. Conflict between them was based 'on a confusion of the images and parables of religion with scientific statement'.

After Einstein, it became disturbingly clear that not only was science unable to provide us with definitive proof, but its findings were inherently limited and provisional. In 1927, Heisenberg formulated the Principle of Indeterminacy in Nuclear Physics, showing that it was impossible for scientists to achieve an objective result because the act of observation itself affected their understanding of the object of their investigation. In 1931, the Austrian philosopher Kurt Gödel (1906–78) devised a theorem to show that any formal logical or mathematical system must contain propositions that were not verifiable within that system; there would always be propositions that could only be proved or disproved by input from outside. This completely undercut the traditional assumption of systematic decidability. In his 1929 Gifford Lectures in Edinburgh, the American philosopher John Dewey (1859–1952) argued that Descartes' quest for certainty could no longer be the goal of modern philosophy. Heisenberg had liberated us from seventeenth-century mechanics, when the universe had seemed like a giant machine made up of separate components, whereas this new generation of scientists was revealing the deep interconnectedness of all reality.

Apparently our brains were incapable of achieving total certainty or incontrovertible proof. Our minds were limited and some problems, it seemed, would remain insoluble. As the American physicist Percy Bridgman (1882–1961) explained:

> The structure of nature may eventually be such that our processes of thought do not correspond to it sufficiently to permit us to think about it at all . . .

> The world fades out and eludes us . . . We are con-
> fronted with something truly ineffable. We have
> reached the limit of the great pioneers of science,
> the vision, namely, that we live in a sympathetic
> world in that it is comprehensible to our minds.

Scientists were beginning to sound like apophatic theologians. Not only was God beyond the reach of the human mind, but the natural world was also terminally elusive. It seemed that a degree of agnosticism was endemic to the human condition.

Yet however unsettling this new scientific revolution, physicists did not seem unduly dismayed. Einstein had declared that if his theory of relativity was correct, it was possible to make three predictions: it would account for the apparently eccentric precession of the planet Mercury; it would be possible to calculate the exact deflection of a beam of light by the gravitational mass of the sun; and because the mass of the sun would reduce the velocity of light, this would have an effect on the light it emitted. Within ten years, the first two predictions were confirmed by experimental data. But the third was not confirmed until the 1960s, because the reduction of the speed of light was minute and scientists lacked the technology to measure it. In principle, Einstein could be proved wrong. He himself was not perturbed: when asked what would happen if his theories were not vindicated in the laboratory, he retorted: 'So much the worse for the experiments; the theory is right!' Scientific theory did not seem to depend wholly on ratiocination and calculation: intuition and a sense of beauty and elegance were also important factors. And during these forty years, physicists were content to work as though relativity were true. They had what religious people would call 'faith' in it. It was finally rewarded when a new spectroscopic technique became available and scientists could finally observe the effect Einstein had predicted. In science, as in theology, human beings could make progress on unproven ideas, which worked practically even if they had not been demonstrated empirically.

The scientific revolution of the 1920s clearly influenced the work of Karl Popper. In his seminal book *The Logic of Scientific Discovery* (1934), he upheld the rationality of science and its commitment to rigorous testing and principled neutrality, but argued that it did not, as commonly thought, proceed by the systematic and cumulative collection of empirically verified facts. It moved forward when scientists came up with bold, imaginative guesses that could never be perfectly verified and were no more reliable than any other 'belief', because testing could only show that a hypothesis was *not* false. Popper was often heard to say: 'We don't know anything.'

According to the British philosopher Bryan Magee, he believed that this was 'the most important philosophical insight there is, which ought to inform all our philosophical activity'. Human beings never achieved perfect knowledge, because anything we know at any given moment is invariably revised later. But far from being depressed by this, Popper found his constant engagement with insoluble problems an endless delight. 'One of the many great sources of happiness,' he explained in his memoir, 'is to get a glimpse, here and there, of a new aspect of the incredible world we live in, and of our incredible role in it.'

This was also Einstein's experience. The new science was no longer averse to mystical wonder and mystery. As Einstein explained:

The most beautiful emotion we can experience is the mystical. It is the sower of all true art and science. He to whom this emotion is a stranger . . . is as good as dead. To know that what is impenetrable to us really exists, manifesting itself to us as the highest wisdom and the most radiant beauty, which our dull faculties can comprehend only in their most primitive forms – this knowledge, this feeling is at the centre of all true religiousness. In this sense, and in this sense only, I belong to the ranks of devoutly religious men.

Einstein emphatically did not subscribe to the personalised modern God. But many theologians – Origen, the Cappadocians, Denys and Aquinas – would have understood exactly what he meant.

NOT EVERYBODY WAS ready to abandon the quest for certainty. During the 1920s, a group of philosophers in Vienna met to discuss, among other topics, the ideas of the Austrian mathematician Ludwig Wittgenstein (1889–1951). The goal of his extremely complex *Tractatus Logico-Philosophicus* (1921) was to show the utter futility of speaking of ideas that lay beyond clear facts based on empirical sense data: 'Whereof one cannot speak,' he said famously, 'thereof one must be silent.' It was quite legitimate to say 'It is raining', because this statement was easy to verify. But it was pointless to discuss anything hypothetical or ineffable – in philosophy, ethics, aesthetics, logic or mathematics – so this type of speculation should be scrapped. True to his principles, Wittgenstein had left his university in 1918 to become a village schoolmaster until 1930, when he accepted a Cambridge fellowship.

The Vienna Circle agreed that because we could make meaningful statements only about matters that could be tested and verified by sense experience, the natural sciences alone were a reliable source of knowledge. Emotive language was meaningless, because it was equipped simply to arouse feeling or inspire action and could not be proved one way or the other. Obviously the concept of 'God' had no meaning at all; indeed, atheism or agnosticism were incoherent positions, because there was nothing to be agnostic or atheistic about. Like other intellectuals at this time, the Logical Positivists – as these philosophers became known – were attempting to return to irreducible fundamentals. Their stringent position also revealed the intolerant tendency of modernity that would characterise other types of fundamentalism. Their narrow definition of truth entailed a wholesale dismissal of the humanities and a refusal to entertain any rival view. Yet human beings have always pondered questions that are not capable of definitive solutions: the contemplation of beauty, mortality and suffering has been an essential part of human experience, and to many it seems not only arrogant but unrealistic to dismiss it out of hand.

At the other extreme of the intellectual spectrum, a form of Christian positivism developed that represented a grass-roots rebellion against modern rationalism. On 9 April 1906, the first congregation of Pentecostalists claimed to have experienced the Spirit in a tiny house in Los Angeles, convinced that it had descended upon them in the same way as upon

Jesus' disciples on the Jewish festival of Pentecost, when the divine presence had manifested itself in tongues of fire and given the apostles the ability to speak in strange languages. When they spoke in 'tongues', Pentecostalists felt they were returning to the fundamental nub of religiosity that exists beneath any logical exposition of the Christian faith. Within four years, there were hundreds of Pentecostal groups all over the United States and the movement had spread to fifty other countries. At first they were convinced that their experience heralded the Last Days: crowds of African-Americans and disadvantaged whites poured into their congregations in the firm belief that Jesus would soon return and establish a more just society. But after the First World War had shattered this early optimism, they saw their gift of tongues as a new way of speaking to God: had not St Paul explained that when Christians found prayer difficult, 'the Spirit itself intercedes for us with groans that exist beyond all utterance?'

In one sense, this was a distorted version of apophatic spirituality: Pentecostalists were reaching out to a God that existed beyond the scope of speech. But the classical apophaticism of Origen, Gregory of Nyssa, Augustine, Denys, Bonaventure, Aquinas and Eckhart had been suspicious of this type of experiential spirituality. At a Pentecostal service, men and women fell into tranced states, were seen to levitate and felt that their bodies were melting in ineffable joy. They saw bright streaks of light in the air and sprawled on the ground, felled by a weight of glory. It was a form of positivism, because Pentecostalists relied on the immediacy of sense experience to validate their beliefs. But the meteoric explosion of this type of faith indicated widespread unhappiness with the modern rational ethos. It developed at a time when people were beginning to have doubts about science and technology, which had shown their lethal potential during the Great War. Pentecostalists were also reacting against the more conservative Christians who were trying to make their Bible-based religion entirely reasonable and scientific.

As A. C. Dixon, one of the founding fathers of Protestant fundamentalism, explained in 1920: 'I am a Christian because I am a Thinker, a Rationalist, a Scientist.' His faith depended upon 'exact observation and correct thinking'. Doctrines were not theological speculations but facts. Evangelical Christians still aspired to the early-modern ideal of absolute certainty based on scientific verification. Yet fundamentalists would also see their faith experiences – born-again conversions, faith healing, and strongly felt emotional conviction – as positive verification of their beliefs. Dixon's almost defiant rationalism indicates, perhaps, a hidden fear. With the Great War, an element of terror had entered conservative Protestantism in the United States. Many believed that the catastrophic encounters at the Somme and Passchendaele were the battles that, according to scripture, would usher in the Last Days; many Christians were now convinced that they were on the front line of an apocalyptic war against Satan. The wild propaganda stories of German atrocities seemed proof positive that they had been right to oppose the nation that had spawned the Higher Criticism. But they were equally mistrustful of democracy, which carried overtones of the 'mob rule' and 'red republic' that had erupted in the atheistic Bolshevik revolution (1917). These American Christians no longer saw Jesus as a loving saviour; rather, as the leading conservative Isaac M. Haldeman proclaimed, the Christ of Revelation 'comes forth as one who no longer seeks either friendship or love . . . He descends that he may shed the blood of men.'

Every single fundamentalist movement that I have studied in Judaism, Christianity and Islam is rooted in profound fear. For Dixon and his conservative Protestant colleagues, who were about to establish the first fundamentalist movement of modern times, it was a religious variation of the widespread malaise that followed the Great War, and it made them distort the tradition they were trying to defend. They were ready for a fight, but the conflict might have remained in their own troubled minds had not the more liberal Protestants chosen this moment to launch an offensive against them. The liberals were appalled by the apocalyptic fantasies of the conservatives. But instead of criticising them on biblical and doctrinal grounds, they hit quite unjustifiably below the belt. Their assault reflected the acute anxieties of the post-war period and, at this time of national trauma, was calculated to elicit outrage, fury and a determination to retaliate.

Fundamentalism – be it Jewish, Christian or Muslim – nearly always begins as a defensive movement; it is usually a response to a campaign of co-religionists or fellow countrymen that is experienced as inimical and invasive. In 1917, during a particularly dark period of the war, liberal theologians in the Divinity School of the University of Chicago launched a media offensive against the Moody Bible Institute on the other side of town. They accused these biblical literalists of being in the pay of the Germans and compared them to atheistic Bolsheviks. Their theology was, according to the *Christian Register*, 'the most astounding mental aberration in the field of religious thinking'. The conservatives responded in kind, retorting that, on the contrary, it was the pacifism of the liberals that had caused America to fall behind in the arms race; it was they who had been in league with the Germans, since the Higher Criticism that the liberals admired had caused the collapse of decent values in Germany. For decades, the Higher Criticism had been surrounded with a nimbus of evil. This type of symbolism, which takes the debate beyond the realm of logic and dispassionate discussion, is a persistent feature of fundamentalist movements.

In 1920, Dixon, Reuben Torrey and William B. Riley officially established the World's Christian Fundamentals Association to fight for the survival of both Christianity and the world. That same year, at a meeting of the Northern Baptist Convention, Curtis Lee Lewis defined the 'fundamentalist' as a Christian who fought to regain territory already lost to the Antichrist and 'to do battle royal for the fundamentals of the faith'. The movement spread. Three years later, the fundamentalists were riding high and it seemed as if they would succeed in gaining the upper hand in most of the Protestant denominations. But then a new campaign caught their attention, which brought fundamentalism, at least for a few decades, into disrepute.

In 1920, the Democratic politician William Jennings Bryan (1860–1925) launched a crusade against the teaching of evolution in schools and colleges; almost single-handedly, Bryan was responsible for ousting the Higher Criticism from the top of the fundamentalist agenda and putting Darwinism in its place. He saw the two issues as indissolubly linked but regarded evolution as by far the more dangerous. Two books – *Headquarters Nights* (1917) by Vernon L. Kellogg and *The Science of Power* (1918) by Benjamin Kidd – had made a great impression on him. The authors had reported interviews with German soldiers, who had testified to the influence that Darwinian ideas had played in Germany's determination to declare war. This 'research' convinced Bryan that evolutionary theory heralded the collapse of morality and decent civilisation. His ideas were naïve, simplistic and incorrect, but people were beginning to be suspicious of science and he found a willing audience. When Bryan toured the United States, his lecture 'The Menace of Darwinism' drew large crowds and got extensive media coverage. But an unexpected development in the south threw the campaign into even greater prominence.

At this date, the fundamentalist movement was chiefly confined to the northern states, but southerners had become concerned about evolution. In 1925, the state legislatures of Florida, Mississippi, Tennessee and Louisiana passed laws to prohibit the teaching of evolution in the public schools. In response, John Scopes, a young teacher in Dayton, Tennessee, decided to strike a blow for free speech, confessed that he had broken the law, and in July 1925 was brought to trial. The new American Civil Liberties Union (ACLU) sent a team of lawyers to defend him, headed by the rationalist campaigner Clarence Darrow (1857–1938). When Bryan agreed to speak in defence of the anti-evolution law, the trial ceased to be about civil liberties and became a contest between Religion and Science.

Like many fundamentalist disputes, the Scopes Trial was a clash between two incompatible points of view. Both Darrow and Bryan represented core American values: Darrow, of course, stood for intellectual liberty and Bryan for the rights of the ordinary folk, who were traditionally leery of learned experts, had no real understanding of science, and felt that sophisticated elites were imposing their own values on small-town America. In the event, Bryan was a disaster on the stand and Darrow was able to argue brilliantly for the freedom that was essential to the scientific enterprise. At the end of the trial, Darrow emerged as the hero of lucid rational thought, while Bryan was seen as a bumbling, incompetent anachronism who was hopelessly out of touch with the modern world: he compounded the symbolism by dying a few days after the trial. Scopes was convicted; the ACLU paid his fine; but Darrow and science were the real victors at Dayton.

The press had a field day. Most notably, the journalist H. L. Mencken (1880–1956) denounced the fundamentalists as the scourge of the nation. How appropriate it was, he crowed, that Bryan who loved simple country people, including the 'gaping primates of the upland villages', had ended his days in a 'one-horse, Tennessee village'. Fundamentalists were everywhere: They are 'thick in the mean streets behind the gas works. They are everywhere learning it is too heavy a burden for mortal minds to carry, even the vague pathetic learning on tap in the little red schoolhouse.' They were the enemies of science and freedom and had no legitimate place in the modern world. The author Maynard Shipley argued that if the fundamentalists seized control of the denominations and imposed their bigoted views on the people, America would be dragged back to the Dark Ages.

At Dayton, the liberals had felt threatened when the rights of free speech and free inquiry were in jeopardy. These rights were sacred, not because they were 'supernatural' but because they were now central to the modern identity, and as such inviolable and non-negotiable. Take these rights away, and everything would be awry. For the fundamentalists, who feared modernity and knew that some of its most vocal exponents had vowed to destroy religion, the new doctrine of biblical inerrancy, proposed by the Princeton theologians, was sacred, not just because of its supernatural sanction but because it provided the sole guarantee of certainty in an increasingly uncertain world. There would in the future be similar clashes between people at different stages of the modernisation process who had competing notions of the sacred. The religious had struck a blow for a value that they felt was imperilled and the liberals had struck back, hard. And at first the liberal assault appeared to have paid off. After the Scopes Trial, the fundamentalists went quiet and seemed suitably vanquished. But they had not gone away. They had simply withdrawn defensively, as fundamentalists of other traditions would do in the future, and created an enclave of Godliness in a world that seemed hostile to religion, forming their own churches, broadcasting stations, publishing houses, schools, universities and Bible colleges. In the late 1970s, when this countercultural society had gained sufficient strength and confidence, the fundamentalists would return to public life, launching a counteroffensive to convert the nation to their principles.

During their time in the political wilderness, the fundamentalists became more radical, nursing a deep grievance against mainstream American culture. Subsequent history would show that when a fundamentalist movement is attacked, it almost invariably becomes more aggressive, bitter and excessive. Rooted as fundamentalism is in a fear of annihilation, its adherents see any such offensive as proof that the secular or liberal world is indeed bent on the elimination of religion. Jewish and Muslim movements would also conform to this pattern. Before Scopes, fundamentalists tended to be on the left of the political spectrum, willing to work with socialists and liberals in the disadvantaged areas of the rapidly industrialising cities. After Scopes, they swung to the far right, where they have remained.

The ridicule of the press proved to be counterproductive, since it made the fundamentalists even more militant in their views. Before Scopes, evolution had not been an important issue; even such ardent literalists as Charles Hodge knew that the world had existed for a lot longer than the six thousand years mentioned in the Bible. Only a very few subscribed to the so-called 'creation science', which argued that Genesis was scientifically sound in every detail. Most fundamentalists were Calvinists, though Calvin himself had not shared their hostility to scientific knowledge. But after Dayton, an unswerving biblical literalism became central to the fundamentalist mindset and creation science became the flagship of the movement. It would become impossible to discuss the issue rationally, because evolution was no longer merely a scientific hypothesis but a 'symbol' indelibly imbued with the misery of defeat and humiliation. The early history of the first fundamentalist movement of the modern era proved to be paradigmatic. When attacking a religion that seems obscurantist, critics must be aware that this assault is likely to make it more extreme.

THE SECOND WORLD War (1939–45) revealed the terrifying efficiency of modern violence. The explosion of atomic bombs over Hiroshima and Nagasaki laid bare the nihilistic self-destruction at the heart of the brilliant achievements of *Homo technologicus.* Our ability to harm and mutilate one another had kept pace with our extraordinary economic and scientific progress and we seemed to lack either the wisdom or the means to keep our aggression within safe and appropriate bounds. Indeed, the shocking discovery that six million Jews had been systematically slaughtered in the Nazi camps, an atrocity that had originated in Germany, a leading player in the Enlightenment, called the whole notion of human progress into question.

The Holocaust is sometimes depicted as an eruption of pre-modern barbarism; it is even seen as an expression of religious impulses that had been repressed in secular society. But historians and social critics have challenged this view. It is certainly true that Christian anti-Semitism had been a chronic disease in Europe since the time of the Crusades; and that while individual Christians protested against the horror and tried to save their Jewish neighbours, many of the denominations were largely and shamefully silent. Hitler had never officially left the Catholic Church and should have been excommunicated; Pius XII neither condemned nor distanced himself from the Nazi programmes.

But to blame the entire catastrophe on religion is simply – and perhaps even dangerously – inaccurate. Far from being in conflict with the rational pursuit of well-organised, goal-oriented modernity, the hideous efficiency of the Nazis was a supreme example of it. Rulers had long initiated policies of ethnic cleansing when setting up their modern, centralised states. In order to use all the human resources at their disposal and maintain productivity, governments had found it necessary to bring out-groups such as the Jews into the mainstream, but the events of the 1930s and 1940s showed that this tolerance was merely superficial and that the old bigotry still lurked beneath. To carry out their programme of genocide, the Nazis relied on the technology of the industrial age: the railways, the advanced chemical industry, and rationalised bureaucracy and management. The camp replicated the factory, the hallmark of industrial society, but what they mass-produced was death. Science itself was implicated in the eugenic experiments carried out there. The modern idolatry of nationalism had so idealised the German *volk* that there was no place for the Jews: born of the new 'scientific' racism, the Holocaust was the ultimate in social engineering in what has been called the modern 'garden culture', which simply eliminated weeds – the supreme, perverted example of rational planning in which everything is subordinated to a single, clearly defined objective.

Perhaps the Holocaust was not so much an expression as a perversion of Judaeo-Christian values. As atheists had been eager to point out, the symbol of God had marked the limit of human potential. At the heart of the Nazi ideology was a romantic yearning for a pre-Christian German paganism that they had never properly understood, and a negation of the God who, as Nietzsche had suggested, put a brake on ambition and instinctual 'pagan' freedom. The extermination of the people who had created the God of the Bible was a symbolic enactment of the death of God that Nietzsche had proclaimed. Or perhaps the real cause of the Holocaust was the ambiguous afterlife of religious feeling in Western culture and the malignant energies released by the decay of the religious forms that had channelled them into more benign, productive outlets. In Christian theology, hell had traditionally been defined as the absence of God, and the camps uncannily reproduced the traditional symbolism of the inferno: the flaying, racking, whipping, screaming and mocking, the distorted bodies, the flames and stinking air all evoked the imagery of hell depicted by the artists, poets and dramatists of Europe. Auschwitz was a dark epiphany, providing us with a terrible vision of what life is like when all sense of the sacred is lost and the human being – whoever he or she may be – is no longer revered as an inviolable mystery.

The Holocaust survivor and Nobel Prize winner Elie Wiesel believed that God died in Auschwitz. During his first night in the camp, he had watched the black smoke curling into the sky from the crematorium where the bodies of his mother and sister were being consumed. 'Never shall I forget those moments,' he wrote years later, 'which murdered my God and my soul and turned my dreams to dust.' He relates how one day the Gestapo hanged a child with the face of a 'sad-eyed angel', who was silent and almost calm as he climbed the gallows. It took the child nearly an hour to die in front of the thousands of spectators who were forced to watch. Behind Wiesel, one of the prisoners muttered: 'Where is God? Where is He?' And Wiesel heard a voice within him saying in response: 'Where is He? Here He is – He is hanging here on this gallows.'

This story can also be seen as an outward sign of the death of God announced by Nietzsche. How do

we account for the great evil we see in a world sup-
posedly created and governed by a benevolent deity?
For the American Jewish writer Richard Rubenstein,
this conception of God is no longer viable. Because
Jews so narrowly escaped extermination, Rubenstein does not believe that they should jettison
their religion, as this would cut them off from their
past. But the nice, moral God of liberal Jews seems
too anodyne and antiseptic: it ignores life's inherent
tragedy in the hope that things will improve. Instead,
Rubenstein is drawn to the self-emptying God of
Isaac Luria, who had not been able to control the
world he had brought into being. The mystics had
seen God as Nothingness; Auschwitz had revealed
the abysmal emptiness of life, and the contemplation
of Luria's En Sof was a way of entering into the pri-
mal Nothingness from which we came and to which
we all return. The British theologian Louis Jacobs,
however, believed that Luria's impotent God could
not give meaning to human existence. He preferred
the classic solution that God is greater than human
beings can conceive and that his ways are not our
ways. God may be incomprehensible, but people have
the option of putting their trust in this ineffable God
and affirming *a* meaning, even in the midst of
meaninglessness.

Another Auschwitz story shows people doing precisely that. Even in the camps, some of the inmates

continued to study the Torah and observe the festivals, not in the hope of placating an angry deity but because they found, by experience, that these rituals helped them to endure the horror. One day a group of Jews decided to put God on trial. In the face of such inconceivable suffering, they found the conventional arguments utterly unconvincing. If God was omnipotent, he could have prevented the Shoah; if he could not stop it, he was impotent; and if he could have stopped it but chose not to, he was a monster. They condemned God to death. The presiding rabbi pronounced the verdict, then went on calmly to announce that it was time for the evening prayer. Ideas about God come and go, but prayer, the struggle to find meaning even in the darkest circumstances, must continue.

The idea of God is merely a symbol of indescribable transcendence and has been interpreted in many different ways over the centuries. The modern God – conceived as powerful Creator, First Cause, supernatural personality realistically understood and rationally demonstrable – is a recent phenomenon. It was born in a more optimistic era than our own and reflects the firm expectation that scientific rationality could bring the apparently inexplicable aspects of life under the control of reason. This God was indeed, as Feuerbach suggested, a projection of humanity at a time when human beings were

achieving unprecedented control over their environment and thought they were about to solve the
mysteries of the universe. But many feel that the
hopes of the Enlightenment also died in Auschwitz.
The people who devised the camps had imbibed the
classical nineteenth-century atheistic ethos that
commanded them to think of themselves as the only
absolute; by making an idol of their nation, they felt
compelled to destroy those they viewed as enemies.
Today we have a more modest conception of the powers of human reason. We have seen too much evil in
recent years to indulge in a facile theology that says –
as some have tried to say – that God knows what he
is doing; that he has a secret plan that we cannot
fathom; or that suffering gives men and women the
opportunity to practise heroic virtue. A modern theology must look unflinchingly into the heart of a
great darkness and be prepared, perhaps, to enter
into the cloud of unknowing.

AFTER THE SECOND World War, philosophers and
theologians all struggled with the idea of God, seeking to rescue it from the literalism that had made it
incredible. In doing so, they often revived older, pre-
modern ways of thinking and speaking about the
divine. In his later years, Wittgenstein changed his
mind. He no longer believed that language should
merely state facts, but acknowledged that words also

issued commands, made promises and expressed emotion. Turning his back on the early modern ambition to establish a single method of arriving at truth, Wittgenstein now maintained that there were an infinite number of social discourses. Each one was meaningful – but only in its own context. So it was a grave mistake 'to make religious belief a matter of evidence in the way that science is a matter of evidence', because theological language worked 'on an entirely different plane'. Positivists and athe-ists who applied the norms of scientific rationality and common sense to religion and those theolo-gians who tried to prove God's existence had all done 'infinite harm', because they implied that God was an external fact – an idea that was intolerable to Wittgenstein. 'If I thought of God as another being outside myself, only infinitely more powerful,' he insisted, 'then I would regard it as my duty to defy him.' Religious language was essentially symbolic; it was 'disgusting' if interpreted literally, but symbol-ically it had the power to manifest a transcendent reality in the same way as the short stories of Tol-stoy. Such works of art did not argue their case or produce evidence, but somehow called into being the ineffable reality they evoked. But because the transcendent reality was ineffable – 'wonderful beyond words' – we would never come to know God merely by talking about him. We had to change our behaviour, 'try to be helpful to other people' and leave egotism behind. If, Wittgenstein believed, he would one day be capable of making his entire nature bow down 'in humble resignation to the dust', then, he thought, God would, as it were, come to him.

The German philosopher Martin Heidegger had no time for the modern, personalised God but saw *Sein* ('Being') as the supreme reality. It was not *a* being, so bore no relation to any reality that we knew; it was wholly other and should more accurately be called Nothing. And yet, paradoxically, Being was *seiender* ('being-er'), more complete than any particular being. Despite its utter transcendence, we could gain some understanding of it – but not through the aggressive thrust of scientific investigation. Instead, we had to cultivate what Heidegger called 'primordial thinking', a listening, receptive attitude, characterised by silence. This was not a logical process and it was not something that we *did*. Instead, it was something that happened within us, a lighting up – almost a revelation. Being was not a fact that we could grasp once and for all, but an apprehension that we built up over time, repetitively and incrementally. We had to immerse ourselves in this cast of mind again and again, in rather the same way as a historian projects himself repeatedly into a historical figure or era.

Theologians, Heidegger believed, had reduced God

to a mere being. God had become Someone Else and theology a positive science. In his early work, therefore, Heidegger insisted that it was essential systematically to dismantle faith in this 'God' so that we might recover a sense of Being. The God of the Philosophers, a typically modern invention, was as good as dead: it was impossible to pray to such a God. This was a time of great depletion; the technological domination of the earth had brought about the nihilism foretold by Nietzsche, because it had made us forgetful of Being. But in his later work, Heidegger found it heartening that God had become incredible. People were becoming conscious of a void, an absence at the heart of their lives. By practising meditative 'thinking', we could learn to experience what Heidegger called 'the return of the holy'. No longer hopelessly mired in mere beings, we should cultivate that primordial waiting in which Being could, as it were, 'speak' to us directly.

Many were dismayed by Heidegger's apparent refusal to condemn National Socialism after the war. But his ideas were extremely evocative and influenced a generation of Christian theologians. Rudolf Bultmann (1884–1976) insisted that God must be de-objectified and that the scriptures did not convey factual information but could only be understood if Christians involved themselves existentially with their faith. 'To believe in the cross of Christ does not mean to concern ourselves ... with an objective event,' he explained, 'but rather to make the cross our own.' Europeans had lost the sense that their doctrines were mere gestures towards transcendence. Their literalist approach showed a complete misunderstanding of the purpose of myth, which is 'not to present an objective picture of the world as it is ... Myth should be interpreted not cosmologically but ... existentially.' Biblical interpretation could not even begin without personal engagement, so scientific objectivity was as alien to religion as to art. Religion was only possible when people were 'stirred by the question of their own existence and can hear the claim that the text makes'. A careful examination of the Gospels showed that Jesus did not see God as 'an object of thought or speculation', but as an existential demand, a 'power that constrains man to decision, who confronts him in the demand for good'. Like Heidegger, Bultmann understood that the sense of the divine was not something to be grasped once and for all; it came to us repetitively by constant attention to the demands of the moment. He was not speaking of an exotic mystical experience. Having lived through the Nazi years, Bultmann knew how frequently in such circumstances, men and women are confronted by an internal demand that seems to come from outside themselves and which they cannot reject without denying what is most authentic to them. God was, therefore, an absolute claim that drew people beyond self-interest and egotism into transcendence.

Paul Tillich (1886–1965) was born in Prussia and served as an army chaplain in the trenches during the First World War, after which he suffered two major breakdowns. After the war, he became a professor of theology at the University of Frankfurt but was expelled by the Nazis in 1933 and emigrated to the United States. He saw the modern God as an idolatry that human beings must leave behind.

> The concept of a 'Personal God', interfering with natural events, or being 'an independent cause of natural events' makes God a natural object beside others, an object among others, a being among beings, maybe the highest, but nevertheless, *a* being. This indeed is not only the destruction of the physical system but even more the destruction of any meaningful idea of God.

A God who interfered with human freedom was a tyrant, not so different from the human tyrants who had wrought such havoc in recent history. A God envisaged as a person in a world of his own, an 'ego' relating to a 'thou', was simply *a* being. Even the Supreme Being was just another being, the final item in the series. It was, Tillich insisted, an 'idol', a human construction that had become absolute. As recent history had shown, human beings were chronically predisposed to idolatry. The 'idea that the human mind is a perpetual manufacturer of idols is one of the deepest things which can be said about our thinking of God', Tillich remarked. 'Even orthodox theology is nothing other than idolatry.' An atheism that passionately rejected a God that had been reduced to a mere being was a religious act.

For centuries, symbols such as 'God' or 'providence' enabled people to look through the ebb and flow of temporal life to glimpse Being itself. This helped them to endure the terror of life and the horror of death, but now, Tillich argued, many had forgotten how to interpret the old symbolism and regarded it as purely factual. Hence these symbols had become opaque; transcendence no longer shone through them. When this happened, they died and lost their power, so when we spoke of these symbols in a literal manner, we made statements that were inaccurate and untrue. That was why, like so many pre-modern theologians, Tillich could state without qualification: 'God does not exist. He is being itself beyond essence and existence. Therefore to argue that God exists is to deny him.' This was not, as many of his contemporaries believed, an atheistic statement:

We can no longer speak of God easily to anybody, because he will immediately question: 'Does God exist?' Now the very asking of that question signifies that the symbols of God have become meaningless. For God, in the question, has become one of the innumerable objects in time and space which may or may not exist. And this is not the meaning of God at all.

God could never be an object of cognition, like the objects and people we see all around us. To look through the finite symbol to the reality – the God beyond 'God' that lies beyond theism – demands courage; we have to confront the dead symbol to find *'the God who appears when God has disappeared in the anxiety of doubt'.*

Tillich liked to call God the ground of being. Like the *atman* in the *Upanishads,* which was identical with the Brahman as well as being the deepest core of the individual self, what we call 'God' is fundamental to our existence. So a sense of participation in God does not alienate us from our nature or the world, as the nineteenth-century atheists had implied, but returns us to ourselves. Like Bultmann, however, Tillich did not regard the experience of Being as an exotic state. It was not distinguishable from any of our other affective or intellectual experiences, because it pervaded and was inseparable from them, so it was inaccurate to say: 'I am now having a "spiritual" experience.' An awareness of God did not have a special name of its own but was fundamental to our ordinary emotions of courage, hope or despair. Tillich also called God the 'ultimate concern'; like Bultmann, he believed that we experienced the divine in our absolute commitment to ultimate truth, love, beauty, justice and compassion – even if it required the sacrifice of our own life.

The Jesuit philosopher Karl Rahner (1904–84), who had been Heidegger's pupil, dominated Catholic thought in the mid twentieth century. He insisted that theology was not a set of dogmas, handed down mechanically as self-evidently true. These teachings must be rooted in the actual conditions in which men and women lived, reflecting the manner in which they knew, perceived and experienced reality. People did not come to know what God was by solving doctrinal conundrums, proving God's existence or engaging in an abstruse metaphysical quest, but by becoming aware of the workings of their own nature. Rahner was advocating a version of what the Buddha had called 'mindfulness'. When we struggle to make sense of the world, we constantly go beyond ourselves in our search for understanding. Thus every act of cognition and every act of love is a transcendent experience because it compels us to reach beyond the prism of selfhood. Constantly, in our everyday experience, we stumble against something that takes us beyond ourselves, so transcendence is built into the human condition.

Rahner stressed the importance of mystery, which was simply an aspect of humanity. The transcendent is not an add-on, something separate from normal existence, because it simply means 'to go beyond'. When we know, choose and love other beings in this world, we have to go outside ourselves; when we try to get beyond all particular beings, we move towards what lies beyond words, concepts and categories. That mystery, which defies description, is God. Religious doctrines were not meant to explain or define the mystery; they were simply symbolic. A doctrine articulates our sense of the ineffable and makes us aware of it. A dogmatic statement, therefore, is 'merely the means of expressing a being referred beyond itself and anything imaginable'.

Bernard Lonergan (1904–84), a Canadian Jesuit, rejected the Positivists' belief that all reliable knowledge was derived from external sense data. In *Insight: A Study of Human Understanding* (1957), he argued that knowledge required more than simply 'taking a look'. It demanded in-sight, an ability to see into an object and contemplate it in its various modes: mathematical, scientific, artistic, moral and finally metaphysical. Continually we find that something eludes us: it urges us to move on further if we wish to become wise. In all cultures, humans have been seized by the same imperatives – to be intelligent, responsible, reasonable and loving, and, if necessary, to change. All this pulls us into the realm of the transcendental, the Real and Unconditioned, which in the Christian world is called 'God'. But this demonstration of the ubiquity of God does not force acceptance. Lonergan concluded by pointing out that his book had merely been a set of signs that readers must appropriate and make their own, a task that each person could only complete for him- or herself.

SINCE THE SCIENTIFIC revolution of the 1920s, there has been a growing conviction that unknowing is an ineradicable part of our experience. In 1962, the American intellectual Thomas Kuhn published *The Structure of Scientific Revolutions*, which criticised Popper's theory of the systematic falsification of existing scientific theories but also undermined the older conviction that the history of science represented a linear, rational and untrammelled progress towards an ever more accurate achievement of objective truth. Kuhn believed that the cumulative testing of hypotheses was only part of the story. During 'normal' periods, scientists did indeed research and test their theories, but instead of reaching out towards new truth, they were in fact simply seeking confirmation of the scientific paradigm of the day. Teachers and texts all worked to support the prevailing orthodoxy and tended to ignore anything that challenged it; they could advance no further than the current paradigm, which thus acquired a conviction and rigidity that was not unlike theological dogma. But then – as had occurred during the 1920s – the 'normal' period was succeeded by a dramatic paradigm shift. The accumulating uncertainties and puzzling results of experiments became irresistible and scientists contended with each other to find a new paradigm. This was not a rational process; it consisted of imaginative and unpredictable flights into the unknown, all influenced by metaphors, imagery and assumptions drawn from other fields. Kuhn seemed to suggest that aesthetic, social, historical and psychological factors were also involved, so that the ideal of 'pure science' was a chimera. Once the fresh paradigm had been established, another 'normal' period would begin, in which scientists worked to endorse the new model, disregarding hints that it was not impregnable, until the next major breakthrough.

It seemed that the scientific knowledge that had come upon the early modern world with the force of a new revelation was not after all fundamentally different from the understanding we derived from the humanities. In *Knowing and Being,* Michael Polyani

(1891–1976), a chemist and philosopher of science, argued that all knowledge was tacit rather than objectively and self-consciously acquired. He drew attention to the role of practical knowledge, which had been greatly overlooked in the modern emphasis on theoretical understanding. We learn how to swim or dance without being able to explain precisely how it is done. We recognise a friend's face without being able to specify exactly what it is that we recognise. Our perception of the external world is not a mechanical, straightforward absorption of data. We integrate a vast number of things into a focal awareness, subjecting them to an interpretive framework that is so deeply rooted that we cannot make it explicit. The speed and complexity of this integration easily outstrips the relatively ponderous processes of logic or inference. Indeed, knowledge is of little use to us until it has been made tacit. Once we have learned how to drive a car, 'the text of the manual is shifted to the back of the driver's mind and transported almost entirely to the tacit operations of a skill'.

When we learn a skill, we literally dwell in the innumerable muscular actions we perform without fully knowing how we achieve them. All understanding, Polyani claimed, is like this. We interiorise a language or a poem 'and make ourselves dwell in them. Such extensions of ourselves develop new faculties in us; our whole education operates in this way; as each of us interiorises the cultural heritage, she grows into a person seeing the world and experiencing life in terms of this outlook.' This, is not dissimilar to the Cappadocians' insistence that the knowledge of God was acquired not merely cerebrally but by the physical participation in the liturgical tradition of the Church, which initiated people into a form of knowing that was silent and could not be clearly articulated.

Polyani argued that the scientific method is not simply a matter of progressing from ignorance to objectivity; as in the humanities, it is more likely to consist of a more complex movement from explicit to tacit knowledge. In order for their investigations to work, scientists often have to believe things that they know will be later proved wrong – though they can never be sure which of their current convictions will be so jettisoned. Because there is so much that cannot be proven, there will always be an element of what religious people call 'faith' in science – the kind of faith that physicists showed in Einstein's theory of relativity in the absence of empirical proof.

Scientific rationalism consists largely of problem-solving, an approach that does lead to systematic advance: after a problem has been solved, it can be laid aside and scientists can move on to tackle the next. But the humanities do not function in this way, because the problems they confront, such as mortality, grief, evil or the nature of happiness, are not capable of a once-and-for-all-time solution. It can take a lifetime's engagement with a poem before it reveals its full depth. This type of contemplation may function differently from ratiocination but it is not for that reason irrational; it is like the 'thinking' that Heidegger prescribed: repetitive, incremental and receptive. The French philosopher Gabriel Marcel distinguishes between a *problem*, 'something met which bars my passage' and 'is before me in its entirety', and a *mystery*, 'something in which I find myself caught up, and whose essence is not before me in its entirety'. We have to remove a problem before we can proceed but we are compelled to participate in a mystery – rather as the Greeks flung themselves into the rites of Eleusis and grappled with their mortality. 'A mystery is something in which I am myself involved,' Marcel continued, 'and it can therefore only be thought of as *a sphere where the distinction between what is in me and what is before me loses its meaning and its essential validity.*' It is always possible – and perhaps a modern temptation – to turn a mystery into a problem and try to solve it by applying the appropriate technique. It is significant that today a detective story based on such problem-solving is popularly known as a 'mystery'. But for Marcel, this is a 'fundamentally vicious proceeding' which could be symptomatic of a 'corruption of the intelligence'.

Philosophers and scientists were beginning to return to a more apophatic approach to knowledge. But the tradition of Denys, Thomas and Eckhart had been so submerged during the modern period that most religious congregations were unaware of it. They tended still to think about God in the modern way, as an objective reality, 'out there', that could be categorised like any other being. During the 1950s, for example, I learned by heart this answer to the question 'What is God?' in the Roman Catholic catechism: 'God is the supreme spirit, who alone exists of himself and is infinite in all perfections.' Denys, Anselm and Aquinas were probably turning in their graves. The catechism had no hesitation in asserting that it was possible simply to draw breath and *define*, a word that literally means 'to set limits upon', a transcendent reality that must exceed all words and concepts.

Not surprisingly, many thoughtful people were unable to believe in this remote and abstractly conceived deity. By the middle of the twentieth century, it was commonly imagined that secularism was the coming ideology and that religion would never again play a role in public life. But atheism was still not perceived as an easy option. Jean-Paul Sartre (1905–80) spoke of a God-shaped hole in human consciousness, where the sacred had always been. The desire for what we call God is intrinsic to human nature, which cannot bear the utter meaninglessness of the cosmos. We have invented a God to explain the inexplicable; it is a divinised humanity. But even if God existed, Sartre claimed, it would be necessary to reject him, since this God negates our freedom. This was not a comfortable creed. It demanded a bleak acceptance of the fact that our lives had no meaning – a heroic act that brought an apotheosis of freedom but also a denial of an intrinsic part of our nature.

Albert Camus (1913–60) could no longer subscribe to the nineteenth-century dream of a deified humanity. Our lives were rendered meaningless by our mortality, so any philosophy that tried to make sense of human existence was a delusion. We had to do without God and pour all our loving solicitude and care upon the world. But this would bring no liberation. In *The Myth of Sisyphus* (1942), Camus showed that the abolition of God required a lifelong and hopeless struggle that was impossible to rationalise. In his passion for life and hatred of death, Sisyphus, king of ancient Corinth, had defied the gods, and his punishment was to spend eternity engaged in a futile task: each day he had to roll a boulder up a mountainside; but when he reached the summit, the rock rolled downhill, so the next day he had to begin all over again. This was an image of the absurdity of human life, from which even death offered no release. Can we be happy in the knowledge that we are defeated before we even begin? If we make a heroic effort to create our own meaning in the face of death and absurdity, Camus concludes, happiness is possible:

> I leave Sisyphus at the foot of the mountain! One always finds one's burden again. But Sisyphus teaches the higher fidelity that negates the gods and raises rocks. He too concludes that all is well. This universe henceforth without a master seems to him neither sterile nor futile. Each atom of that stone, each mineral flake of that night-filled mountain, in itself forms a world. The struggle itself toward the heights is enough to fill a man's heart. One must imagine Sisyphus happy.

By the middle of the twentieth century, many found it impossible to imagine that getting rid of God would lead to a brave new world; there was no serene Enlightenment optimism in the rationality of human existence. Camus had embraced the state of unknowing. He did not know for certain that God did not exist; he simply chose to believe this. We have to live with our ignorance in a universe that is silent in the face of our questioning.

But within a decade of Camus' death, the world

had drastically changed. There was a rebellion against the ethos of modernity; new forms of religiosity, a different kind of atheism, and, despite the fact that unknowing seemed built into our condition, a strident lust for certainty.

Death of God

DURING THE 1960s, Europe experienced a dramatic loss of faith. After a rise in religious observance during the austerity years immediately after the Second World War, for example, British people stopped going to church in unprecedented numbers and the decline has steadily continued. A recent poll has estimated that only about six per cent of Britons attend a religious service regularly. During the sixties, in both Europe and the United States, sociologists proclaimed the triumph of secularism. In 1965, *The Secular City*, a best-seller by the American theologian Harvey Cox, claimed that God was dead, and that henceforth religion must centre on humanity rather than a transcendent deity; if Christianity failed to absorb these new values, the churches would perish. The decline of religion was just one sign of major cultural change during this decade when many of the institutional structures of modernity were pulled down: censorship was relaxed; abortion and homosexuality were legalised; divorce became easier; the women's movement campaigned for gender equality; and the young railed against the modern ethos of their parents. They called for a more just and equal society, protested against the materialism of their governments, and refused to fight in their nation's wars or to study in its universities. They created an 'alternative society' in revolt against the mainstream.

Some saw the new wave of secularism as the fulfilment of the rational ethos of the Enlightenment. Others saw the 1960s as the beginning of the end of the Enlightenment project and the start of 'Postmodernity'. Truths hitherto regarded as self-evident were called into question: the teachings of Christianity, the subordination of women and the structures of social and moral authority. There was a new scepticism about the role of science, the modern expectation of continuous progress and the Enlightenment ideal of rationality. The modern dualities of mind/body, spirit/matter and reason/emotion were challenged. Finally, the 'lower orders', who had been marginalised and even subjugated during the modern period – women, homosexuals, blacks, indigenous populations, the colonised peoples – were demanding and beginning to achieve liberation.

As the philosopher Nietzsche had predicted, the idea of God had simply died and for the first time ordinary folk, who were not pioneering scientists or philosophers, were happy to call themselves atheists. They did not spend time examining the scientific and rational arguments against God's existence: for many Europeans, God had simply become *otiosus*. As the political philosophers Antonio Negri and Michael Hardt have explained:

> Modern negativity is located not in any transcendent realm but in the hard reality before us: the fields of patriotic battles in the First and Second World Wars, from the killing fields at Verdun to the Nazi furnaces and the swift annihilation of thousands in Hiroshima and Nagasaki, the carpet bombing of Vietnam and Cambodia, the massacres from Setif and Soweto to Sabra and Shatila, and the list goes on and on. There is no Job who can sustain such suffering.

Belief had emerged as the enemy of peace. John Lennon's song 'Imagine' (1971) looked forward to a world where there was no Heaven and no Hell – 'above us only sky'. The elimination of God would solve the world's problems. This was a simplistic belief, since many of the conflicts that had inspired the peace movement were caused by an imbalance of political power, secular nationalism, and the struggle for world domination. But religion had been implicated in many of these atrocities; in Northern Ireland and the Middle East it had served as a tribal or ethnic marker; it was used rhetorically by politicians; and it was clear that it had signally failed in its mandate of saving the world.

In the United States, a small group of theologians created a form of 'Christian atheism' that tried to engage with the 'hard reality' of world events and enthusiastically proclaimed the death of God. In *The Gospel of Christian Atheism* (1966), Thomas J. J. Alitzer announced the 'good news': God's demise had freed us from slavery to a tyrannical transcendent deity. Altizer spoke in mystical, poetic terms of the dark night of the soul, the pain of abandonment, and the silence that must ensue before what we mean by 'God' can become meaningful once more. Our former notions of divinity had to die before theology could be reborn. In *The Secular Meaning of the Gospel* (1963), Paul Van Buren argued that science and technology had invalidated traditional mythology. Even the sophisticated theology of Bultmann or Tillich was still immersed in the old, unviable ethos. We must give up God and focus on Jesus of Nazareth, the liberator, who 'defines what it is to be a man'. William Hamilton saw Death of God theology as a twentieth-century way of being Protestant in *Radical Theology and the Death of God* (1966): just as Luther had left his cloister and gone out into the world, the modern Christian must walk away from the sacred place where God used to be; he would find the man Jesus in the world of technology, power, money, sex and the city. Human beings did not need God; they must find their own solution to the world's problems.

The Death of God movement was flawed: it was essentially a white, middle-class, affluent and – sometimes offensively – Christian theology. Like Hegel, Altizer saw the Jewish God as the alienating deity that had been negated by Christianity. Black theologians asked how white people felt able to affirm freedom through God's death when they had enslaved people in God's name. But despite its limitations, Death of God theology was a prophetic voice calling for a critique of contemporary idols (which included the modern idea of God) and urging a leap from familiar certainties into the unknown that was in tune with the spirit of the sixties.

But despite its vehement rejection of the authoritarian structures of institutional religion, sixties youth culture was demanding a more religious way of life. Instead of going to church, the young went to Kathmandu or sought solace in the meditative techniques of the Orient. Others found transcendence in drug-induced trips, or personal transformation by such techniques as the Erhard Seminars Training (EST). There was a hunger for *mythos* and a rejection of the scientific rationalism that had become the new Western orthodoxy. Much twentieth-century science had been cautious, sober and highly conscious, in a disciplined, principled way, of its limitations and areas of competence. But since the time of Descartes, science had also been ideological and had refused to countenance any other method of arriving at truth. During the sixties, the youth revolution was in part a protest against the illegitimate domination of rational discourse and the suppression of *mythos* by *logos*. But because the understanding of the traditional ways of arriving at more intuitive knowledge had been neglected in the West during the modern period, the sixties quest for spirituality was often wild, self-indulgent and unbalanced.

IT WAS, THEREFORE, premature to speak of the death of religion, and this became evident in the late 1970s, when confidence in the imminent arrival of the Secular City was shattered by a dramatic religious resurgence. In 1978–9, the world watched in astonishment as an obscure Iranian ayatollah brought down the regime of Shah Muhammad Reza Pahlavi (1919–80), which had seemed to be one of the most progressive and stable states in the Middle East. At the same time as governments applauded the peace initiative of President Anwar al-Sadat of Egypt (1918–81), observers noted that young Egyptians were donning Islamic dress, casting aside the freedoms of modernity, and engaging in a takeover of university campuses in order to reclaim them for religion – in a way that was paradoxically reminiscent of student rebellions during the sixties. In Israel, an aggressively religious form of Zionism (which had originally been a defiantly secular movement) had risen to political prominence and the ultra-Orthodox parties, which David Ben-Gurion (1886–1973), Israel's first prime minister, had confidently predicted would fade away once the Jewish people had their own secular state, were gathering strength. In the United States, Jerry Falwell founded the Moral Majority in 1979, urging Protestant fundamentalists to get involved in politics and to challenge any state or federal legislation that pushed a 'secular humanist' agenda.

This militant religiosity, which would emerge in every region where a secular, Western-style government had separated religion and politics, is determined to drag God and/or religion from the sidelines to which they have been relegated in modern culture and back to centre-field. It reveals a widespread disappointment in modernity. Whatever the pundits, intellectuals or politicians thought, people all over the world were demonstrating that they wanted to see religion more clearly reflected in public life. This new form of piety is popularly known as 'fundamentalism', but many objected to having this Christian term foisted on to their reform movement. They do not in fact represent an atavistic return to the past. These are essentially innovative movements and could have taken root at no time other than our own. Fundamentalisms too can be seen as part of the post-modern rejection of modernity. They are not orthodox and conservative; indeed, many are actually anti-orthodox, and regard the more conventional faithful as part of the problem.

These movements have mushroomed independently and even those that have emerged within the same tradition do not have an identical vision. However, they bear what has been called a 'family resemblance', and seem instinctively to follow the pattern set by American Protestant fundamentalism, the earliest of these movements. All are initially defensive movements rooted in a profound fear of annihilation, which causes them to develop a paranoid vision of the 'enemy'. They begin as intrafaith movements and only at a secondary stage, if at all, do they direct their attention to a foreign foe.

Protestant fundamentalism was chiefly exercised by theological questions that had been challenged by the new scientific discoveries. Fundamentalisms in other traditions have been sparked by entirely different problems and are not preoccupied with 'belief' in the same way. In Judaism, the state of Israel has inspired every one of the Jewish fundamentalisms, because this has been the form in which secularism has chiefly impacted on Jewish religious life. Some are passionately *for* the state of Israel and regard its army, political institutions and every inch of the Holy Land as sacred; others are either vehemently *opposed* to the notion of a secular state or adopt a deliberately neutral stance towards it. In the Muslim world, the political state of the *ummah*, the 'community', has become an Achilles heel. The Qur'an insists that the prime duty of a Muslim is to build a just and decent society, so when Muslims see the *ummah* exploited or even terrorised by foreign powers and governed by corrupt rulers, they can feel as religiously offended as a Protestant who sees the Bible spat upon. Islam has traditionally been a religion of success: in the past, Muslims were always able to surmount disaster and use it creatively to rise to new spiritual and political heights. The Qur'an assures them that if their society is just and egalitarian, it will prosper – not because God is tweaking history on their behalf but because this type of government is in line with the fundamental laws of existence. But Muslims have been able to make little headway against the secular West and some have found this as threatening as Darwinism seems to fundamentalist Christians. Hence there have been ever more frantic efforts to get Islamic history back on track.

Because fundamentalists feel under threat, they are defensive and unwilling to entertain any rival point of view, yet another expression of the intolerance that has always been part of modernity. Christian fundamentalists take a hard line on what they regard as moral and social decency. They campaign against the teaching of evolution in public schools, are fiercely patriotic but averse to democracy, see feminism as one of the great evils of the day, and conduct a crusade against abortion. Some extremists have even murdered doctors and nurses who work in abortion clinics. Like evolution, abortion has become symbolic of the murderous evil of modernity. Christian fundamentalists are convinced that their doctrinal 'beliefs' are an accurate, final expression of sacred truth and that every word of the Bible is literally true – an attitude that is a radical departure from mainstream Christian tradition. They believe that miracles are an essential hallmark of true faith and that God will give the believer anything that he asks for in prayer.

Fundamentalists are swift to condemn people whom they regard as the enemies of God: most Christian fundamentalists see Jews and Muslims as destined for hellfire and some regard Buddhism, Hinduism and Daoism as inspired by the devil. Jewish and Muslim fundamentalists take a similar stance, each seeing their own tradition as the only true faith. Muslim fundamentalists have toppled governments and some extremists have been guilty of terrorist atrocities. Jewish fundamentalists have founded illegal settlements in the West Bank and the Gaza Strip with the avowed intention of driving out the Arab inhabitants, convinced that they are paving the way for the Messiah; others throw stones at Israelis who drive their cars on the Sabbath.

In all its forms, fundamentalism is a fiercely reductive faith. In their anxiety and fear, fundamentalists often distort the tradition they are trying to defend. They can, for example, be highly selective in their reading of scripture. Christian fundamentalists quote extensively from the Book of Revelation and are inspired by its violent End-time vision, but rarely refer to the Sermon on the Mount, where Jesus tells his followers to love their enemies, to turn the other cheek and not to judge others. Jewish fundamentalists rely heavily on the Deuteronomist sections of the Bible and seem to pass over the rabbis' injunction that exegesis should lead to charity. Muslim fundamentalists ignore the pluralism of the Qur'an and extremists quote its more aggressive verses to justify violence, pointedly disregarding its far more numerous calls for peace, tolerance and forgiveness. Fundamentalists are convinced that they are fighting for God, but in fact this type of religiosity represents a retreat from God. To make purely human, historical phenomena – such as 'Family Val-ues', 'the Holy Land' or 'Islam' – sacred and absolute values is idolatry and, as always, their idol forces them to try to destroy its opponents.

But it is essential for critics of religion to see fun-damentalism in historical context. Far from being typical of faith, it is an aberration.

Epilogue

WE HAVE GOT used to thinking that religion should provide us with information. Is there a God? How did the world come into being? But this is a modern aberration. Religion was never supposed to provide answers to questions that lay within the reach of human reason. That was the role of *logos*. Religion's task, closely allied to that of art, was to help us to live creatively, peacefully and even joyously with realities for which there were no easy explanations and problems that we could not solve: mortality, pain, grief, despair, and outrage at the injustice and cruelty of life. Over the centuries, people in all cultures discovered that by pushing their reasoning powers to the limit, stretching language to the end of its tether, and living as selflessly and compassionately as possible, they experienced a transcendence that enabled them to affirm their suffering with serenity and courage. Scientific rationality can tell us why we have cancer; it can even cure us of our disease. But it cannot assuage the terror, disappointment and sorrow that come with the diagnosis, nor can it help us to die well. That is not within its remit. Religion will not work automatically, however; it requires a great deal of effort and cannot succeed if it is facile, false, idolatrous or self-indulgent.

Religion is a practical discipline, and its insights are not derived from abstract speculation but from spiritual exercises and a dedicated lifestyle. Without such practice, it is impossible to understand the truth of its doctrines. This was also true of philosophical rationalism. People did not go to Socrates to learn anything – he always insisted that he had nothing to teach them – but to have a change of mind. Participants in a Socratic dialogue discovered how little they knew and that the meaning of even the simplest proposition eluded them. The shock of ignorance and confusion represented a conversion to the philosophic life, which could not begin until you realised that you knew nothing at all. But even though it removed the last vestiges of the certainty upon which people had hitherto based their lives, the Socratic dialogue was never aggressive; rather it was conducted with courtesy, gentleness and consideration. If a dialogue aroused malice or spite, it would fail. There was no question of forcing your interlocutor to accept your point of view: instead, each offered his opinion as a gift to the others and allowed them to alter his own perceptions. Socrates, Plato and Aristotle, the founders of Western rationalism, saw no opposition between reason and the transcendent. They understood that we feel an imperative need to drive our reasoning powers to the point where they can go no further and segue into a state of unknowing that is not frustrating but a source of astonishment, awe and contentment.

Religion was not an easy matter. We have seen the immense effort made by yogins, *hesychasts*, Kabbalists, exegetes, rabbis, ritualists, monks, scholars, philosophers and contemplatives, as well as lay people in regular liturgical observance. All were able to achieve a degree of *ekstasis* that, by introducing us to a different kind of knowing, 'drives us out of ourselves'. In the modern period too, scientists, rationalists and philosophers have experienced something similar. Einstein, Wittgenstein and Popper, who had no conventional religious 'beliefs', were quite at home in this hinterland between rationality and the transcendent. Religious insight requires not only a dedicated intellectual endeavour to get beyond the 'idols of thought' but also a compassionate lifestyle that enables us to break out of the prism of selfhood. Aggressive *logos*, which seeks to master, control and kill off the opposition, cannot bring this transcendent insight. Experience proved that this was only possible if people cultivated a receptive, listening attitude, not unlike the way we approach art, music or poetry. It required *kenosis*, 'negative capability', 'wise passiveness' and a heart that 'watches and receives'.

The consistency with which the various religions have stressed the importance of these qualities indicates that they are somehow built into the way men and women experience their world. If the religious lose sight of them, they are revived by poets, novelists and philosophers, that does not mean that one is 'right' and the others 'wrong'. On this matter, nobody can have the last word. All faith systems have been at pains to show that the ultimate cannot be adequately expressed in any theoretical system, however august, because it lies beyond the reach of words and concepts.

But many people today are no longer comfortable with this apophatic reticence. They feel that they know exactly what they mean by God. The Catechism definition I learned at the age of eight – 'God is the Supreme Spirit, who alone exists of himself and is infinite in all perfections' – was not only dry, abstract and rather boring but it was also incorrect. The process that should have led to a stunned appreciation of an 'otherness' beyond the reach of language ended prematurely. The result is that many of us have been left stranded with an incoherent concept of God. We learned about God at about the same time as we were told about Santa Claus. But while our understanding of the Santa Claus phenomenon evolved and matured, our theology remained some-what infantile. Not surprisingly, when we attained intellectual maturity, many of us rejected the God we had inherited and denied that he existed.

We now understand basic religious terms differently and in a way that has made faith problematic. 'Belief' no longer means 'trust, commitment and engagement' but has become an intellectual assent to a somewhat dubious proposition. Religious leaders often spend more time enforcing doctrinal conformity than devising spiritual exercises that will make these official 'beliefs' a living reality in the daily lives of the faithful. Instead of using scripture to help people to move forward and embrace new attitudes, people quote ancient scriptural texts to prevent any such progress. The words 'myth' and 'mythical' are now often synonymous with untruth. 'Mystery' no longer refers to a ritualised initiation but has been routinely decried as mental laziness and incomprehensible mumbo-jumbo. The Greek fathers used the word *dogma* to describe a truth that could not be put readily into words, could only be understood after long immersion in ritual, and, as the understanding of the community deepened, changed from one generation to another. Today in the West, 'dogma' is defined as 'a body of opinion formulated and authoritatively stated', while a 'dogmatic' person is one who 'asserts opinions in an arrogant and authoritative manner'. We no longer understand Greek *theoria* as the activity of 'contemplation' but as a 'theory', an idea in our heads that has to be proved. This neatly demonstrates our modern understanding of religion as something that we think rather than something that we do.

In the past, religious people were open to all manner of different truths. Jewish, Christian and Muslim scholars were ready to learn from pagan Greeks who had sacrificed to idols, as well as from each other. It is simply not true that science and religion were always at daggers drawn: in England, the Protestant and Puritan ethos were felt to be congenial to early-modern science and helped its advance and acceptance. Mersenne, who belonged to a particularly austere branch of the Franciscan order, took time off from his prayers to conduct scientific experiments and his mathematical ideas are still discussed today. The Jesuits encouraged the young Descartes to read Galileo and were fascinated by early-modern science. Indeed, it has been said that the first scientific collective was not the Royal Society but the Society of Jesus. But as modernity advanced, confidence dimmed and attitudes hardened. Thomas Aquinas had taught Aristotelian science when it was controversial to do so and had studied Jewish and Muslim philosophers while most of his contemporaries reflexively supported the Crusades. But the Church later interpreted his theology with a rigidity that he would have found repugnant. The modern Protestant doctrine of the literal infallibility of scripture was first formulated in the 1870s when scientific methods of biblical criticism were undermining 'beliefs' held to be factually true. Like the new and highly controversial Catholic doctrine of papal infallibility, defined in 1870, it expressed a yearning for absolute certainty at a time when this was proving to be a chimera.

Today, when science itself is becoming less determinate, it is perhaps time to return to a theology that asserts less and is more open to silence and unknowing. Here perhaps dialogue with the more thoughtful Socratic forms of atheism can help to dismantle ideas that have become idolatrous. In the past, people were often called 'atheists' when society was in transition from one religious perspective to another: Euripides and Protagoras were accused of 'atheism' when they denied the Olympian gods in favour of a more transcendent theology; the first Christians and Muslims, who were moving away from traditional paganism, were persecuted as 'atheists' by their contemporaries. When we have eaten a strong-tasting dish in a restaurant, we are often offered a sorbet to cleanse our palate so that we can taste the next course properly. An intelligent atheistic critique could help us to rinse our minds of the more facile theology that is impeding our understanding of the divine. We may find that for a while we have to go into what mystics called the dark night of the soul or the cloud of unknowing. This will not be easy for people used to getting instant information at the click of a mouse. But the novelty and strangeness of this negative capability could surprise us into awareness that stringent ratiocination is not the only means of acquiring knowledge. It is not only a poet like Keats who must, while waiting for new inspiration, learn to be 'capable of being in uncertainties, Mysteries, doubts, without any irritable reaching after fact & reason'.

From almost the very beginning, men and women have repeatedly engaged in strenuous and committed religious activity. They evolved mythologies, rituals and ethical disciplines that brought them intimations of holiness that seemed in some indescribable way to enhance and fulfil their humanity. They were not religious simply because their myths and doctrines were scientifically or historically sound, because they sought information about the origins of the cosmos, or merely because they wanted a better life in the hereafter. They were not bludgeoned into faith by power-hungry priests or kings: indeed, religion often helped people to oppose tyranny and oppression of this kind. The point of religion was to live intensely and richly here and now. Religious people are ambitious. They want lives overflowing with significance. They have always desired to integrate with their daily lives the moments of rapture and insight that came to them in dreams, in their contemplation of nature, and in their intercourse with one another and with the animal world. Instead of being crushed and embittered by the sorrow of life, they sought to retain their peace and serenity in the midst of their pain. They yearned for the courage to overcome their terror of mortality; instead of being grasping and mean-spirited, they aspired to live generously, large-heartedly and justly and to inhabit every single part of their humanity. Instead of being a mere workaday cup, they wanted, as Confucius suggested, to transform themselves into a beautiful ritual vessel brimful of the sanctity that they were learning to see in life. They tried to honour the ineffable mystery they sensed in each human being and create societies that honoured the stranger, the alien, the poor and the oppressed. Of course they often failed. But overall they found that the disciplines of religion helped them to do all this. Those who applied themselves most assiduously showed that it was possible for mortal men and women to live on a higher, divine or godlike plane and thus wake up to their true selves.

One day a Brahmin priest came across the Buddha

sitting in contemplation under a tree and was aston-
ished by his serenity, stillness and self-discipline.
The impression of immense strength channelled
creatively into an extraordinary peace reminded
him of a great tusker elephant. 'Are you a god, sir?'
the priest asked. 'Are you an angel . . . or a spirit?' No,
the Buddha replied. He explained that he had simply
revealed a new potential in human nature. It was
possible to live in this world of conflict and pain at
peace and in harmony with one's fellow creatures.
There was no point in merely believing it; you would
only discover its truth if you practised his method,
systematically cutting off egotism at the root. You
would then live at the peak of your capacity, activate
parts of the psyche that normally lie dormant, and
become fully enlightened human beings. 'Remember
me,' the Buddha told the curious priest, 'as one who
is awake.'

© Michael Lionstar

KAREN ARMSTRONG is one of the world's leading commentators on religious affairs. She spent seven years as a
Roman Catholic nun, but left her teaching order in 1969
to read English at St Anne's College, Oxford. In 1982,
she became a full time writer and broadcaster. She is a
best-selling author of over sixteen books. A passionate
campaigner for religious liberty, Armstrong has addressed
members of the United States Congress and participated
in the World Economic Forum. In 2013 she received the
British Academy's inaugural Nayef Al-Rodhan Prize for
improving transcultural understanding.

Her books include *Through the Narrow Gate* (1982), *A History of God* (1993); *In the Beginning: A New Interpretation
of Genesis* (1996); *Islam: A Short History* (2000); *The Battle
for God* (2000); *The Spiral Staircase* (2004); *The Case for
God* (2009); *Twelve Steps to a Compassionate Life* (2010);
Fields of Blood (2014) and *The Lost Art of Scripture* (2019).

RECOMMENDED BOOKS BY KAREN ARMSTRONG

A History of God
In the Beginning
Twelve Steps to a Compassionate Life

THE CASE FOR GOD

There is widespread confusion about the nature
of religious truth. For the first time in history,
a significantly large number of people want nothing
to do with God. Militant atheists preach a
gospel of godlessness with the zeal of missionaries
and find an eager audience.

Does God have a future? Karen Armstrong examines
how we can build a faith that speaks to the needs of
our troubled and dangerously polarised world.

'Prodigiously sourced, passionately written'
Financial Times

'A journey through religion that helps us to rescue what
remains wise from so much that to many in Britain
today no longer seems true . . . Armstrong is one
of the handful of wise and supremely intelligent
commentators on religion' Alain de Botton, *Observer*

'Forget Richard Dawkins – just read it with an
open mind' Jeanette Winterson

FIELDS OF BLOOD: RELIGION AND THE HISTORY OF VIOLENCE

It is the most persistent myth of our time: religion is the cause of all violence. But history suggests otherwise. Karen Armstrong, former Roman Catholic nun and one of our foremost scholars of religion, speaks out to disprove the link between religion and bloodshed. *Fields of Blood* is a celebration of the ancient religious ideas and movements that have promoted peace and reconciliation across millennia of civilisation.

'Karen Armstrong's wonderful book certainly cleanses the mind. It may even do a little repair work on the heart' Ferdinand Mount, *Spectator*

'Elegant and powerful, erudite and accurate . . . dazzling in its breadth and historical detail' *Washington Post*

'Mind-boggling . . . we feel we are in the hands of an expert. Armstrong is doing us a great service' *Guardian*

THE LOST ART OF SCRIPTURE

In our increasingly secular world, holy texts are at best seen as irrelevant, and at worst as an excuse to incite violence, hatred and division. So what value, if any, can scripture hold for us today?

But as Karen Armstrong shows in this fascinating journey through millennia of history, this narrow reading of scripture is a relatively recent phenomenon. For hundreds of years these texts were seen as fluid and adaptable, rather than a set of rules or a 'truth' that has to be 'believed'.

Armstrong argues that if scripture is used to engage with the world in more meaningful and compassionate ways, we will find that it still has a great deal to teach us.

'Karen Armstrong is a genius' A.N. Wilson

VINTAGE MINIS

The Vintage Minis bring you the world's greatest writers on the experiences that make us human. These stylish, entertaining little books explore the whole spectrum of life – from birth to death, and everything in between. Which means there's something here for everyone, whatever your story.

vintageminis.co.uk